You're Accepted

A Stress-Free and Proven Approach to Getting Into

College

Katie Malachuk

KAPLAN

PUBLISHING

New York

© 2010 Katie Malachuk

Published by Kaplan Publishing, a division of Kaplan, Inc.
1 Liberty Plaza, 24th Floor
New York, NY 10006

Previously published in hardcover as *You're Accepted* (ISBN: 978-1-60714-124-2).

Library of Congress Cataloging-in-Publication Data

Malachuk, Katie.
  You're accepted : Lose the stress. Discover yourself.
  Get into the college that's right for you / Katie Malachuk.
    p. cm.
  ISBN 978-1-60714-715-2
  1. Universities and colleges--United States--Admission.
  2. College choice--United States. I. Title.
  LB2351.2.M238 2009
  378.1'61--dc22

                                    2009014046

Printed in the United States of America

10 9 8 7 6 5 4 3 2 1

ISBN: 978-1-60714-715-2

Kaplan Publishing books are available at special quantity discounts to use for sales promotions, employee premiums, or educational purposes. For more information or to purchase books, please call the Simon & Schuster special sales department at 866-506-1949.

Praise for *You're Accepted*

"Malachuk's advice is spot on. Colleges want individuals, not clones, and *You're Accepted* provides the tools to help students present themselves powerfully and authentically in the college admission process. With humor and a touch of irreverence, Malachuk asks you to 'believe in yourself.' This is Yoda for a new generation of college-goers."

— **Seth Allen**, Dean of Admission &
Financial Aid, Grinnell College

"It's rare that one can say of the same book, 'Kids, give this to your parents if you want them to understand who you are and where you will thrive and grow into who you were meant to be,' and 'Parents, give this to your kids if you want to participate with them in this most important rite of passage.'"

— **Elizabeth Lesser**, cofounder, Omega Institute, and
New York Times bestselling author of *Broken Open:
How Difficult Times Can Help Us Grow*

"Amid the chaos of college admissions, Malachuk provides a refreshing step-by-step guide on how to maintain a sense of self in the process—the key to getting into the right college for you."

— **Kathleen Kingsbury**,
Time and *Daily Beast* contributor

"This should be required reading for every high school student (and their parents) *before* they begin the college application process."

— **Daniel J. Saracino**, Assistant Provost for
Enrollment, University of Notre Dame

This book is dedicated to you, the reader —

You are the light of the world.

Let it shine!

Table of Contents

INTRODUCTION ix

CHAPTER 1 1

"So Where Do You Want to Go to College?"
(or, "Stop Asking Me that Question!"):
Make Decisions for Yourself and Run Your Own Race

CHAPTER 2 55

What Can I Do to Be More Attractive to Schools?
Follow Your Bliss

CHAPTER 3 99

The Dreaded Essay: Fear Doesn't Stand a Chance
against Self-Discovery

CHAPTER 4 145

Parents, Teachers, Coaches, Friends, Recommenders,
and Even Interviewers: They Really *Can* Help You—
If You Let Them

CHAPTER 5 173

Overcoming Obstacles: Bust through Stress,
Exhaustion, Boredom, and Frustration;
Learn Your Lessons and Keep the Faith

CHAPTER 6 203

The Waiting Game—and Then Decision Time:
You Own Your Life, so Live It *Now*

CHAPTER 7 233

A To-Do List for Higher Level Living:
Five Outward Actions and Five Inward Ideas

FINAL THOUGHTS 249

Joy in the Journey

Namaste. 257

References 265

About the Author 267

Index. 269

Introduction

Here you are. It's a big deal, the applying-to-college thing. It starts to feel like it's the only thing, doesn't it? Like it's the defining moment of your life: this massive challenge of being accepted by your dream schools. But what if you made the challenge much simpler but also much bigger? Could you be so fearless as to make the challenge of applying to college, and possibly all of life, simply being the real *you*?

Colleges say they want candidates to be themselves. Yet being yourself is one of the hardest things to do in life, in practice and on paper. We have so many ideas in our heads about who we *should* be and what we *should* do, not to mention the advice and opinions of parents, friends, teachers, admissions committees, and books (guilty as charged) swirling around us. It's easy to follow your ego down a path of becoming who you think you're supposed to be rather than following the truth of your heart. But as Ralph Waldo Emerson (1841, ¶ 3) said, "Trust thyself: every heart vibrates to that iron string. Insist on yourself; never imitate." Right on, brother.

So I have two goals with this book. I will certainly give you tried-and-true advice on specific aspects of the application process—school selection, competition around tests and grades, extracurriculars, interviews, recommenders, stress, decisions, and especially the essays. More important, though, I hope this book helps you reframe how you look at applying to college. You are embarking on what can be an incredible time to get to know who you are—what you value, what makes you happy, who is important to you, what experiences have shaped you, what dreams you have. Applying to college is a valuable rite of passage to becoming an independent adult. Unfortunately, the focus has become the outcome, the judgment at the end. With this book, I'm hoping you can take back the effort, the process, and own it for yourself. Use this time to become closer to who you really are. Ideally, you can walk away from this process with not only a school acceptance but also a far more precious gift: self-acceptance.

Okay, though, I hear you. You want to get into school! I get it. But when you approach the applications with the goal of self-realization, you'll actually get better results. You'll make smarter choices about where you're applying, searching out schools where you truly fit. Moreover, you are going to present a far deeper, more thoughtful, and thus more attractive application to schools.

So why should you pay any attention to what I have to say? Because before going to business school at Stanford, I was the director of admissions for Teach For America, which is similar to running admissions for a small college. There I found that the best applicants were the ones who truly knew themselves and could show that on paper. More recently, I have been an MBA admissions consultant, and I have worked with college applicants in a pro bono capacity. For years, I have been helping applicants structure their overall application stories, choose schools, create essays, prepare recommenders, practice for interviews, and decide where to go. It's incredibly fun and fulfilling, especially as I've infused tricks of the trade from my other job, teaching yoga, to help these applicants come to know and express themselves on a far deeper level than they'd anticipated going into the process.

Perhaps the best part of all of this is that I have read a gazillion admissions essays and have helped people see that writing them can be a life-changing experience. In addition to advising my clients, I'm constantly giving advice on essays to friends, friends of friends, and children of friends for business school, law school, college…all of it. I consider it an honor to learn about each applicant's challenges and dreams. Call me a geek, but it's an awesome way to get to know people—*if* they truly reveal who they are. And that's how school admissions officers feel, too: candidates who know themselves well make better applicants because you see who they are and want them to light up your campus.

But I also know a lot about this process from my own journey. Although my resume looks polished, the real story hasn't been all that pretty. Here's the fun version of my resume that I can tick off at parties: "I went to Harvard, did Teach For America, and then was the director of admissions for Teach For America, went to Stanford for business school, did strategy consulting and worked for an education start-up, and then ditched office jobs to become a yoga teacher and admissions consultant, and I'm now writing books on applying to schools."

Wow, sounds so smooth and successful. Even the risky part of leaving office jobs worked out, with the yoga teaching and admissions consulting and now writing books. Yeah, well, behind that sound bite is more than a decade of stops and starts; suffering through some serious sadness; feeling totally lost; weeping all over Chicago, D.C., New York City, and much of Northern California; and three stints of living with my parents (the shame!).

You see, I went to two colleges and two graduate schools. By age 29, I had attended Northwestern, Harvard, Georgetown Law School, and Stanford's Graduate School of Business, but I only graduated from Harvard and Stanford. I dropped out of Northwestern and Georgetown. A friend of mine from college, upon hearing that I'd started doing admissions consulting, joked that I was the perfect person to help people get *into* schools, but they should talk to someone else about *staying*. Exactly.

And I'm not going to lie to you: this time that you are in right now, when I applied to colleges, went to Northwestern and dropped out, was one of the lowest, saddest periods in my existence. I did not approach my college applications in a mindful way. As a senior at a big, public high school outside of Washington, D.C., I applied to the same schools everyone else did without thinking about where I would be a good fit. I fixated on getting into Duke because it was really popular, and I saw myself as a complete failure when I got rejected. It didn't help that the day after we got the news from colleges, I walked through my high school A hall only to hear someone say, "Can you *believe* Katie Malachuk didn't get into Duke?" Ouch. We all let our worlds shrink to the college admissions process, and maybe you can relate to that right now. Where you're applying, where you get in, where you're going...it seemed that was all that mattered in life, and I had failed. Rather than leaving high school grateful and excited for the opportunities ahead, I left defeated and anxious about my future.

I was depressed at Northwestern for a lot of reasons, none of which had to do with Northwestern because it's a great school. But one of my biggest issues at the time was this idea of having failed at college admissions, which stuck inside the perfectionist, young adult me. Dropping out of college, taking time off, and transferring to Harvard was a major victory, not because I got into Harvard but because I did some massive soul-searching and came to know and accept myself in an unprecedented way. The greatest gift I got was to see that at Harvard, just as at Northwestern, I had natural ups and downs with classes, extracurriculars, boyfriends, all of it. Sure, Harvard was a better fit for me, and I was in a better place emotionally at that point, but I still had a normal human existence full of joy, sadness, laughter, and tears. The real game in life is trying to *keep it real* and stay grateful through all of it.

And I am extremely grateful for that ride I took through two college admissions processes. That time of falling down and dropping out taught me how to pick myself up and dive back in. "Trees only grow in the valley," as my mom says, and it was in the depths of this sadness and fear that I planted the seeds to live a life that is now full of hope and faith. And living from hope and faith is a way better time.

Of course, I didn't get the self-acceptance lesson in one take;

such is karma, as we'll discuss. So I had a lot of twists and turns throughout my 20s as I tried to find my place in the world. Indeed, my graduate school experiences mirrored the undergraduate in many ways. To borrow from the SAT analogy format: Georgetown Law was to Stanford Business as Northwestern was to Harvard. And leaving more traditional jobs to become a yoga teacher, admissions consultant, and writer has involved more of the same lessons yet again.

But throughout these challenges and joys, I have learned the importance of being authentic, tapping into your intuition, learning your lessons, following your heart, and keeping faith that the universe has much bigger and brighter things in store for you than you can even imagine. These lessons were solidified when I became a yoga teacher and dove into that philosophy and awoke a spiritual side of myself. Don't get freaked out about seeing the word *spiritual*! We'll get into that later (in chapter 5), but really it's just about feeling connected to that piece of you that is beyond your body and your mind, that piece of you that is connected to everything else out there and full of effortless grace and love.

Perhaps as you feel the stress and competition around college applications, you doubt if you have a naturally radiant, patient, compassionate, graceful, and loving part of you. Don't sweat it. We all do. As it turns out, your grandma, your kindergarten teacher, your rabbi, your minister, Jesus, Mohammad, Buddha, Bono, and Oprah are all onto something—you've got a peaceful, joyful, loving, content place inside. We like to bury that glowing *Self*, as we call it in yoga, underneath our chattering human minds, which feed on fear and ego to try and protect us in this sometimes scary, competitive world. Hopefully this book can help you practice seeing that you are much bigger and brighter than those everyday chattering thoughts and unconscious behavior patterns that we all have.

Again, though, this book is *very* much about getting into college and doing that in a thoughtful, reflective way. It's about getting to know the real you underneath all of the labels, assumptions, and roles that you play in the world. This is a book about revealing your heart and understanding that you're already accepted, just for being born you with all of your uniquely fabulous gifts and talents and quirks and challenges. You're here for a far greater purpose than just getting into college. This application process is not the be-all, end-all of your life. It's really just the beginning—the beginning of becoming an independent adult and putting your fantastic Self out into the world. Get ready to be *you*! For real. Get ready to own it and bring it in a big, big way!

❖

CHAPTER 1

"So Where Do You Want to Go to College?" (or, "Stop Asking Me That Question!")

Make Decisions for Yourself and Run Your Own Race

When my oldest brother Danny was a junior in high school, my dad called him into the dining room one Sunday morning. As Danny remembers it, Dad was holding that enormous guide to colleges and said, "Big? Small? Warm? Cold?" A solid opener to the "Where do you want to go to college?" discussion. Danny's first choice was Amherst (small, cold), but he didn't get in. Instead, he went to Bowdoin (also small, cold), where he met his lovely wife. My sister-in-law considered

1

Brown and Tufts because the two boys she liked were interested in those schools; thankfully, she went to Bowdoin and met my brother!

I have one applicant this year who insists on prioritizing good food, so naturally, Cornell made the list. Another applicant just wants someplace "less snotty" than his high school, and Wesleyan seems pretty chill. One applied to Howard and Spellman because it would be nice to have all African-American peers, but she also put Hofstra and Fordham on the list. Another applied to Mount Holyoke because classes of all women could be cool.

Duke was the hot school my senior year, and I desperately wanted to get in there for no real reason other than its hotness. Michigan had rolling admissions, and the idea of an October acceptance was way appealing to many of us. University of Arizona had been ranked best party school or maybe best-looking girls; either way, that got it on some lists. One friend's dad went to Princeton. Another's sister went to UPenn. Someone's longed for ex-boyfriend went to Georgetown. Past crushes of friends went to (in no particular order) Virginia Tech, USC, Northwestern, Stanford, Lehigh, Tulane, Middlebury, and Miami of Ohio. They all ended up on the lists. Some folks wanted to be close to home. Some not so much. One guy thought living in the country would be peaceful. Others were New York City or bust. One girl wanted to major in drama at Carnegie Mellon. An entire clique of girls applied together to West Virginia University. A friend from my childhood swim team wanted to go to a college that was totally different from the small private school she'd attended since first grade, which meant a larger school with a good football team and hot, tall guys. This for her was Boston College.

Clearly, a lot of things are at play when you're choosing your list of colleges. Try asking people who are years past this process how they came up with their list of schools. You'll often get "I don't know," accompanied by a look up into their eyebrows as if they're trying to search their brains for reasons. Sometimes there's a rationale, whether it's beautiful scenery or their mom's alma mater or everyone in honors English applied there. Other times it's pretty random. One friend from Harvard said, "I was utterly clueless about where to apply.... Neither of my parents went to college..., and my mom fully expected me to get married instead of spending any money we didn't have on school. I basically started thinking about schools by buying one of those huge books from the bookstore that listed all of the accredited colleges." And thus we end up back at the enormous guide to colleges. Big? Small? Warm? Cold?

"So where are you applying?" Because it's the first question people ask you, we'll start our journey together by exploring the school choice process in a traditional way—discussing size, geography, diversity, culture, quality of life, academics, extracurriculars, and financing. We'll look at examples from my applicants and friends, and I'll provide a list of questions for each area. It's all presented with the intention of helping you get your creative juices flowing as to how you might want to prioritize schools. Remember, *you* are doing the choosing. What do you want from a college? What is important to you about where you live, your social life, what you'll study, how you'll play? It's really good stuff to know about yourself so you can create a life that actually jibes with who you are. So instead of stressing, maybe you can use this choosing process as a chance to get to know yourself and your needs better.

For most of us, where we apply to college is one of the first, independent, grown-up things we do. You can use this as an opportunity to practice thinking for yourself across your entire life. To that end, we're going to look at how to tap into your intuition to do the considering. Does using intuition sound creepy? It's not. It's just a way to clear out the voices of others that get stuck inside your head so you can begin to make decisions, about colleges and everything else, for yourself.

Finally, we'll look at the competition beast that rears its ugly head as you begin this process. Once you start thinking about schools, you start thinking about everyone else who's applying and comparing yourself. Hopefully, a big takeaway for you from this book is that you should run your own race. To that end, we'll explore feelings around competition and how to pay attention to your reactions and move forward with a focus on doing *your* thang. Alrighty then, here we go.

Size: Little Fish in a Big Pond or a Big Fish in a Little Pond?

Big? Small? Usually I hear adults emphasize the academic ramifications of going to a big school versus a small one. The standard argument is this: Large universities have big classes but more course offerings; they also have famous professors, but the professors are less accessible. Small colleges have smaller classes but fewer offerings, and although they may have less well-known professors, the faculty are very accessible.

Through my work advising business school applicants, I've spoken with hundreds of people about their undergraduate academic experiences. The most important factor in creating an intimate undergraduate academic learning environment with a personalized course of study and access to professors is (drum-roll please) the student's initiative! In other words, it's up to *you* what you get out of your college education. You can go to a small, hand-holding school, flounder around unfocused, and develop not a single relationship with a professor. Like one guy from tiny Hamilton who didn't talk to his professors outside of class, floated through school without engaging in his economics major at all, and emerged admittedly apathetic about academics and his career path. Or you can go to a massive research university, create an individualized major, and walk away with professors as lifelong mentors. Like the guy who went to the enormous University of Michigan, created his own major, and started a successful business with a friend out of their independent study project. He had four professor mentors (four more than most of us!), one of whom hooked him up with a sweet job at Microsoft after graduation. No matter where you go, you can make your academic experience what you want if you're willing to work for it.

Size also comes into play with extracurriculars. It can be exciting and eye opening to have tons of talented classmates, but it can be depressing and defeating when you never get a part in the musical. That said, the extracurricular situation plays out like academic life. It's really up to you. You can do all of the things you want to do at a big school, but you might have to hustle and compete a bit more and maybe not be the star. For my brother Mike, joy at getting a basketball scholarship to the Division I University of Vermont was partly offset by frustration that he wouldn't play that much. At a smaller Division III school, he could have started. He made that choice of more bench time when he chose UVM for the scholarship. On the other hand, though it may be easier to get a starting spot on the basketball team and take on club leadership at a small school, you may not find all of the extracurricular options you want. But you can always start organizations yourself, like one of my business school applicants from Jamaica who founded a reggae club at his small New England college. He was much loved for this contribution!

Many people I know and have worked with found that size had the greatest impact on their social lives. It can feel really cozy and charming to know everyone in your class, but it can feel stifling and claustrophobic when you break up with one of them. When I was going through tough times with my business school boyfriend at Stanford (the business school is really small), a friend joked that we should get a publicist to handle all of the inquiring minds. Not funny. Small schools can feel a wee bit like *Us* magazine in terms of the gossip wheel, but it can be worth it to know all of your classmates and feel like a family. Also, many of the smaller colleges have relationships with nearby schools, so you can expand your world (and date people outside of the paparazzi glare!). The Five Colleges connection among Amherst, Smith, Mount Holyoke, Hampshire, and UMass–Amherst is a good example of this. And fear not, big school fans who also want the family feel. Big schools make themselves smaller through frats and sororities, teams or clubs, your dorm, or any other campus organization you join—even just your circle of friends. You'll make yourself a family of amazing friends no matter where you go.

Here are some questions to consider about size:

- How large was your high school, and how did you feel there?
- If you knew everyone's name and everyone knew your name, did you like that?
- If you didn't know your whole class, did you like that?
- When you're in class, is it easier to pay attention and stay focused if there are fewer people in the room?
- Does it help you understand material if you can answer questions and have discussions during class?
- Can you pay attention even when you're in a large group?
- Does taking notes and quietly processing information help you understand it better? (Note: Even if you go to a big school with big lecture classes, you'll still have small section meetings for debriefing.)
- Were you the captain or leader of teams or clubs? Is that important to you?

+ Did you wish you had more options for extracurriculars?
  Do you like to start things?

+ Do you feel as though you fall into the shadows in a large
  environment? Would you like to push yourself to be out
  in front more?

+ Do you enjoy stepping forward in large groups to take on
  leadership?

Geography and Weather: You May Think It Doesn't Matter— until It Rains Every Weekend

Have you ever seen Santa Barbara, California? It's off-the-charts beautiful. The first time I went there was for a Teach For America conference when I was teaching in Oakland, California. Having gone to college in Chicago and Boston, I had only one thought upon seeing UCSB: *How the heck does anyone do homework here?* Sun, sand, waves…we didn't even make it through the panel discussions at the conference before we took off for the beach. Of course, at Northwestern or Harvard, we tried to do the laid-back thing, shedding our many layers come May (yes, not until May) to read on the shores of Lake Michigan or the banks of the Charles in all our pasty glory. But for the majority of the year, the library was a safe haven from the lashing wind or snowdrifts outside. Yet I have many friends who went to UCSB and other such geographically blessed schools, and they assure me that people do study there. They are super smart and accomplished folks, so you can tell your parents that you will be too after four years as a Rainbow Warrior at University of Hawaii.

From what I've seen with applicants and friends, one of the biggies to think about with geography is whether you want to see something new and be far away from home. For most of us, at some point in our lives, we long to explore a new place, new terrain. Go West, young man, so to speak. College can be an ideal time to do this, but it may not be the right time. A friend's high school girlfriend was dying to get out of New Orleans, which she considered provincial, and hightailed it to Columbia. One girl was desperate to leave busy Miami, and Sarah Lawrence felt like a farm, an oasis from her urban upbringing. One friend from Oregon was so convinced she couldn't get a good education in the state of Oregon that she only applied to East Coast schools (though now she wonders why on earth she thought that about her home state). Another friend from the Bay Area was applying to all East Coast schools until his sister, who went to Wellesley, suggested he stay closer to home. She didn't think he'd like the East. In fact, on his East Coast school tours, none of those places really appealed to him. So he applied and got into Stanford. It was just the right fit, but he'd blown it off initially because it didn't seem adventurous enough.

This may or may not be the right time for your excellent adventure far from your hometown. Think about where you are emotionally and what would feel good, something new or something familiar. There's no right answer. One applicant wanted to be no more than three hours away from New York City, far enough to feel away but close enough to get home if his mom needed him. Or maybe it's your parents who don't want you to go too far. One friend from Long Island really wanted to get away, but her mom said Duke was the furthest she could go. If your heart is set on wandering off to parts more unknown, try to talk honestly with your parents about that. (We'll talk more about you and your parents during this application season in chapter 4.) If they won't budge or if you're not ready to go far away now, know that you'll have plenty of chances while you're at college (with study abroad or exchanges) and after graduation to chart a new course. College is just one chapter. My friend who stayed close to home at Stanford lives in New York now, and the East Coast feels just right at this time in his life.

Also, you might consider whether you want to live in the area where you go to college after you graduate. This is more of a consideration for graduate schools, but it can come into play with your undergraduate choice as well. One of my business school applicants grew up in Los Angeles and went to UCLA for undergrad because at age 18, he already knew that he wanted to work in the entertainment industry. He started building contacts while in college. Another friend went to University of Colorado–Boulder without having any idea of a future career, simply because he knew he wanted to live there after school. Smart guy—it's gorgeous! Or you can try the reverse and use college as a way to live someplace you don't want to settle for the long run. One business school friend went to Dartmouth for a few years of woodsy, skiing fun because she knew she'd live in a city after graduation. Of course, if you don't know where you want to be after college, it makes more sense to choose based on where you want to be right now—also a great move.

But what about the second half of my dad's school selection rubric: Warm? Cold? Weather is hugely important, as it can deeply affect your mood. One friend discovered that the gray winter skies of New Hampshire made him feel as though he took a sad pill every day. For others, sunshine is not a good time. One friend hated her California school because the constant sunshine made her feel bad about pursuing her favorite pastime, holing up in a coffee shop and reading the paper all day. One of my best friends from Harvard was from Hawaii and didn't understand that sunny skies could coexist with cold temperatures. Fall of her freshman year, she'd see bright blue skies out of her dorm window and come running downstairs in shorts and a T-shirt only to meet the surprising chill of Boston in September. Her cousin, also from Hawaii, ended up going to Stanford, an easier transition. People joke about choosing schools based on weather, but it's not to be taken lightly. You don't want to live someplace where you're sad every day just because it's rainy.

And keep in mind seemingly mundane considerations like topography. For example, when my family was touring colleges with my older brother Danny, we went to Williams, and I crossed it off my mental list (as a fifth grader) because the drive through the mountains made me super nauseous. I reconsidered when I saw their double-decker carrels in the library—like tree houses for homework! But the trip out of there confirmed that I'd be absolutely barfy going back and forth to that place. That said, the flatness of the Midwest got to me a little at Northwestern. While it was great for long runs (no hills!), I missed the rolling East Coast landscape. Like weather, the general look of a place can inspire or bum you out, so it's worth thinking about what you want to look at as you procrastinate on papers by staring out of your dorm window.

There's also a city/country/college town consideration. One of my friends at Stanford business school hated having to drive everywhere. She was from New York, and it drove her nuts that she couldn't walk outside and buy milk—she had to get in a car, drive to a store, park, etc. Argh! Some people are just the opposite and can't imagine navigating the public transportation or hustle and bustle of city schools, like one applicant who said that one trip on the subway confirmed New York University was just too much for him. Or maybe you like the Goldilocks "just right" quality of college towns like Ann Arbor, Michigan, which one applicant described as picture book college. Like weather, the city/country/town factor is enormous because it affects your emotions and mood every day, depending on how you like to live and what you like to do socially.

Here are some questions to consider about geography and weather:

- Do cities or busy places energize you or make you tired and want to be alone?

- Do wide-open spaces refresh you or make you feel isolated and removed from the action of life?

- Would you want to stay in the general location of the school after college? (This is a bigger question for graduate school, but it's worth thinking about now, too.)

- When you see yourself going out, do you envision clubs, theaters, and restaurants in a city? Or do you see frat parties, house parties, and local kinds of places?

- Do you need sunshine to feel happy inside?

- Do you love to be outside, hanging out or running, swimming, etc.?

- Do you feel happy in big sweaters sipping cocoa?

- Do you love to slip on flip-flops and be good to go?

- Do you want to deal with having or needing a car?

- Would you prefer to walk everywhere?

Diversity: Getting to Know You, Getting to Know All about You

Hands down, the thing I loved most about Harvard was the diversity of my friends. When I showed my mom a picture of a bunch of us out for dinner before a formal, she exclaimed, "That looks like a UN summit." For all of us, having friends, classmates, roommates, teammates, boyfriends, girlfriends, etc. who were different races and ethnicities allowed us to have refreshingly frank conversations about race, which can be tough to do in our country.

Of course, diversity doesn't just apply to race and ethnicity. You'll learn tons and bust open stereotypes by hanging out with classmates who have different political leanings, sexual preferences, family situations, socioeconomic backgrounds, and international or regional roots. Never again will you be in such a rich and open environment in this regard. Seek it out and soak it up.

One note on diversity, though: make sure you take care of yourself and find a place where you'll be comfortable. I mean that in the broadest of terms, but I'll offer two specific examples. I was working with an applicant who was considering a very small liberal arts school in the Northeast, and she was worried about being one of the few African-American students there. We were looking over the view book and could not find a single black student. In fact, the pictures were all of white people doing the whitest things you've ever seen. Playing Ultimate Frisbee in togas? Really? She grew up in the Bronx, and it just looked too different for her. Not only was the school mostly white, but she was also somewhat concerned about being one of the few black people in the very tiny, very white town. Where would she get her hair done? Would they have restaurants she liked? She turned the school down. Another friend worried about being one of what he guessed would be about ten gay guys at the very small school he was considering. The fact that it was near a major city helped, but it concerned him that he'd feel too different and would have a very limited dating pool. He went anyway.

In any situation where you're wondering what your experience would be like, get in touch with the school. Some schools have organized recruitment events to give you a sense of the experience there. One of my friends from Harvard came very close to going to Brown because she really enjoyed the "Black at Brown" weekend; it felt a long way—in a good way—from her almost entirely white high school. One applicant had ruled out Smith until she went for the minority recruitment weekend. She stayed with a friend's older sister, and the campus felt welcoming and fun. It went back on the list.

Maybe your school of choice doesn't have a particular recruitment effort. You can still do your homework on the clubs and social opportunities there. Contact the school and see if you can email or speak with someone in the South Asian Association, or maybe they have a student rep for the LGBT club. Current students or recent alumni are the best resources on what the scene is like, so maybe you can connect with someone online.

The point is, if you have questions, please ask the admissions/recruitment/student life departments how you can get more information. Don't just make a decision based on a view book picture and assumptions. Talk to people who know the real deal.

Here are some questions to consider about diversity:

- How diverse are your friends right now? How do you feel about that?
- What schools would offer you a more diverse population, if that's what you're seeking?
- If you're part of a minority population, how important is it that your college has a community of peers from the same background?

- What's the makeup of the town/city of the college? Do you want to live there?
- In general, would you feel safe, happy, and comfortable at the school and in the surrounding environment?
- Whom can you speak with about the diversity at the school?

Culture: Different Colleges Have Different "Personalities"

During spring of junior year of high school, a few of my guy friends decided that they were no longer average suburban white boys wearing J. Crew sweaters. They were now liberal, they were progressive, they wanted to break out of the mold. At this point, one of them decided Grinnell would be a great fit for him. He heard it had a left-leaning bent, and even better, no one from our high school was applying there. Suddenly going to a small school in Iowa seemed rebellious, even exotic. He was way into it.

Then he went to visit. When he returned, he humbly said, "I guess I liked it. But I'm not sure if I'm ready to wear a skirt." So he'd seen a dude wearing a skirt. Probably not every guy there was without an inseam, but it was enough to make him question the whole school. He needed to do some more research obviously, but his hesitancy revealed his general ambivalence and gut instinct about his fit with the school. It was maybe too liberal for him.

Doesn't mean it's too liberal for you, or even that it's "liberal" at all. It's all relative.

Culture speaks to the general atmosphere of the school and where it's located. Although I want to emphasize again how important it is to cultivate a diverse crowd at school, you don't want to be someplace where, politically and socially, you're going to feel alienated and miserable. Like I said, though, it's all relative, so two people could read the culture of a school completely differently.

It's really important to do some thinking about what kind of social scene you want. Fraternities and sororities are a big deal on a lot of campuses. One mistake my friends from high school and I made was thinking that if it said 40 percent of the students joined fraternities and sororities, then that was less than half and thus not the dominant social scene. But no. Because so many people were doing their own thing, that 40 percent in the Greek system dominated the organized social scene on campus, for better or worse depending on how you felt about them.

So think about how and where you want to hang out socially. At some schools, you'll go to parties in fraternities or sororities or in houses that students rent. Other places, you'll hang out in dorm rooms. Still other places, you'll be going out in the surrounding city or town. At some schools, your extracurricular affiliations become your social network. Check out the club offerings, which can give you a feel for the place and what students like to do. Once I was at Harvard, I was really grateful that I'd spent a year as a Big Ten sorority girl, so to speak, going to huge tailgates, football games, and frat parties. My Harvard social life felt so different, though it was also full of great parties (especially dance parties, because I was part of a club that taught dance in the public schools). But I felt fortunate to have had both experiences. Talk to older friends or siblings about their experiences, not to copy what they have done but to get a sense of how different scenes feel.

Riffing off the guys-in-skirts example, the styles of dress on campus sometimes give you a feeling of what's the right fit for you. One of the cutest, best-dressed girls at my high school said Georgetown felt too dressy for her. She was turned off by the pearls-with-baseball-caps thing. Similarly, I felt that Northwestern was a little too dressy for me, while Harvard felt just right. But one of my best friends at Harvard said she was initially surprised that people changed into different clothes to go out on Friday nights from the ones they'd worn to classes earlier that day. That wasn't how she rolled at her rural Ohio high school, and she felt a little intimidated at first.

Maybe the clothes thing is silly, but it gives you a feel for the place. And don't take my word for it on any of these particular observations about schools, because that was a long time ago and schools (and styles) change. You'll get a broader sense of the style of the place when you visit or connect with people online.

Here are some questions to consider about culture:

+ Do you like to stand out? Do you like to blend in? Would you do either at this school?

+ What are your political leanings? Would you feel comfortable at the college in this regard? Would you feel comfortable in the surrounding community?

+ Does the school have clubs you'd want to join?

+ Is this a place where you could start clubs of interest to you?

+ How do you like to spend your free time?

+ Does social life revolve around campus events?

+ Do people go to sports games?

+ Do students hang out in dorm rooms? Do they hang out in coffee shops?

+ Do people flock to off-campus parties? Frat parties?

+ What are your thoughts on fraternities and sororities? Can't wait to join one? Curious but not set on the idea? Fine with them, but don't want them to be a part of your world? Couldn't handle being at a school with this type of social scene?

+ Does the campus feel like a connected group?

+ Do people go out in small groups to local places in the surrounding town or city?

Quality of Life: What's for Dinner?

At Harvard, we lived in dorms the entire time with a meal plan. It was so warm and fuzzy that they even had students submit their parents' best recipes, so we had Mike's Mom's Lasagna and

Carrie's Dad's Stir-fry as options. (Quick aside: The best label on any dining hall dish ever was the Chili Con Carne without Meat. Call on your rudimentary Spanish to see the hilarity.) Friends who went to University of Wisconsin or UCLA, or even my brother at Bowdoin, had a completely different experience: they moved off campus by junior year to fend for themselves in terms of cleaning their places and making dinner. What they gained in independence, they lost in convenience. Sometimes that fifth night of Ramen noodles for dinner isn't so appetizing.

Overall, the quality of life at colleges is outstanding. Lovely dorms, great food, spectacular gyms. Middlebury's got a climbing wall! Yale has a sustainable farm! Even if you're commuting to school from home, you can still take advantage of the food and facilities. It's good living all around, and what a treat for you to start thinking about how you want to live. One applicant visited Smith for the weekend and saw that the resident advisor, a junior living in the freshman dorms to help folks out, had her very own common room. "The girl had her own couch. I'm going there!" It's exciting to think about living on your own while still being cared for a bit.

If you're living in dorms, at most schools you'll have an assigned roommate (or a few) your freshman year. I could dedicate an entire book to whack freshman year roommate stories, ranging from the sort of annoying ("He ate all of the NutriGrain bars that my mom sent, even when I hid them.") to the really annoying ("He got wasted and peed on the laundry, the plant, and then me.") to just plain weird ("She was a Wiccan! She thought she was a gnome princess?!?"). But for all of those not-so-great roommate matches, many are wonderful, and many more are tolerable. If you're really bummed out by the idea of living with someone, then take that into consideration when you're looking at schools and living options.

Do put some thinking into on-campus versus off-campus living situations. I really loved being in a dorm my whole time at Harvard for the efficiency and family feel, but I didn't think about that at all when I was applying to schools. A friend who went to Yale felt the same way about dorm life, and he had purposely made those schools his first choices for that reason.

Even if you go the apartment-living route, you may not have to cook all of your meals for yourself. Be sure to do the math on the meal plan stuff. One friend who lived off campus still bought meals on campus but too many. He didn't need all of those on-campus lunches purchased beforehand, so the money was wasted. That may not seem like a big deal, but you don't want to end up paying for meals on campus and paying to eat off campus a lot. You'll be double-paying, and not even Carrie's Dad's Stir-fry is worth paying twice.

Think about your quality of life beyond just sleeping and eating. Consider how you like to take care of yourself in terms of physical activity, artistic endeavors, and spiritual pursuits. It's important to nurture yourself from the inside out and outside in. (We'll talk more about finding balance in chapter 4.) So if painting's not your major but still really important to you, make sure there are art classes or studios on campus or around town. One friend didn't major in art but spent hours blissfully painting away on her Big Ten campus. If rock climbing is your thing, you've got the wall at Middlebury—or check out University of Colorado–Boulder for the real deal. If you go to synagogue every week, make sure there's a campus Hillel. One business school applicant became really involved in his Hillel, and it ended up giving him a lot of leadership experience in addition to nurturing his spirit.

It's these day-to-day things that actually make up your life. You want to feed your soul, fill your belly, and get a good night's sleep so you have the energy to soak in all of the academic, extracurricular, and social aspects of school.

Here are some questions to consider around quality of life:

- Are you cool with eating whatever comes your way? Would you be fine with dorm food all the time? Or do you have strong preferences?

- Do you want to cook for yourself? Do you never want to cook?

- Does a dorm seem fun and full of community?

- Are you dying to have an apartment of your own?

- Would you go nuts with a roommate?

- What kinds of working out do you like to do? Can you do it there?

- What kinds of artistic endeavors lift you up? Do the colleges you're considering have facilities for this?

- Is there something you want to learn how to do? Is that an option at this school?

- How do you nourish the inner you—churches, temples, places to get quiet? Can you do that there?

- Would you feel safe there?

- If you're a commuting student, what's the commute like? Do you want to do that every day?

Extra-curriculars: They School You More than Classes

When I brainstorm with business school applicants for essay examples of leadership, creativity, or simply moments of joy, college extracurriculars top the list. The sports teams, service organizations, newspapers, political clubs, cooking clubs, eating clubs, sororities—they provide favorite moments, as well as important training grounds for being an adult in the world. One applicant saw the power of his words as a future manager when delivering an inspiring speech as captain of the lacrosse team. Another applicant realized her passion for politics by writing for the school paper. One guy awoke his interest in business by fund-raising for a club water polo team. One woman realized the importance of her cultural roots by getting her *bhangra* on with the South Asian Association. One guy loved his a capella group so much that he started one in New York City when he was working after college. Whether your extracurriculars help you tap into a professional interest, allow you to celebrate your artistic side, or simply give you a crew of wonderful friends, they are an essential part of college. (We'll talk much more about this in chapter 2, which discusses how to follow your bliss.)

As you look at schools, check out their extracurricular offerings. See what you want to join and what you want to start yourself (two points we'll discuss more in chapter 3 on the essay). You should never disregard an extracurricular love. This speaks a bit to the geography point as well. If you love University of Texas–Austin but also love to surf, then it may not be the best fit for you. One of my roommates at Northwestern was from Oregon and had been on her high school ski team. She really missed the slopes and joined the Northwestern ski team. As I mentioned before when relating my own topographical woes, there aren't too many hills out there. She didn't last long: "We were skiing behind the Kmart down a hill made of what I believe was trash. I'm done." I'm sure they ski other places, so all you skiing fans set on Northwestern, don't be discouraged. Do your research though, for all of your schools, to see if you can continue your favorite extracurricular pursuits there.

Beyond the extracurriculars you enjoy now, think about those secret dreams of things you haven't started but want to do once you get to college—maybe there will be your chance to try dancing or drawing or tutoring. It's such an important time to develop passions so that you have outlets once you begin your adult, working life. Check to make sure your schools of choice can support those talents and interests bubbling inside you, waiting to come out. You already know what they are, and after the discussion of following your bliss in chapter 2, they will be even more clear.

Here are some questions you should consider around extracurriculars to figure out what's really important to *you*:

- What role have extracurriculars played in your life thus far? How do you feel about that?

- What's important to you about your favorite extracurriculars?

- How do you hope to grow in these areas at school?

- Do you want to lead or even start a club or a group? Does that opportunity seem likely at this school (based on its size or resources)?

- Do you want to be a joiner without the responsibility of leading/founding? Does that seem likely at this school (again, based on its size or resources)?

- What's the culture of the school with regards to extracurriculars?

- What's the level of involvement of students in extracurriculars? Does that match with your expectations for your college life?

- What things must you have in your life to feel balanced and well-rounded? Would you have them at this school, either by enjoying them on your own or joining/starting a group?

- What have you secretly been wanting to try? Can you do this at this school, either by enjoying it on your own or joining/starting a group?

Financial Aid:
Who's Paying Your Tuition, and How?

Alas, college is not a free ride: it comes with a very hefty price tag. This is one of the reasons that choosing schools wisely is so important. You do not want to spend the money on a place where you don't want to be at school. Like a lot of families right now, maybe yours is in a tough financial place. When I started college, my dad had been out of work for a bit, a situation all too prevalent these days. When I was so sad at Northwestern, I felt awful calling home and crying about it to my mom, who had been working in customer service at Nordstrom all day processing underwear returns to pay for my tuition. She would have hated knowing that I felt guilty, because she was thrilled to help with my education, but I couldn't help feeling that I was wasting everyone's time and money if I wasn't happy there. College is probably the biggest investment you will make in your early adult life. You want to make sure that the dollars either you are your parents are spending are indeed well spent.

If you are fortunate enough to have parents who are paying or helping with the costs, it's good to have a discussion with them about how much they can afford and what you can do to help. (Again, more on your relationship with your parents in chapter 4.) One applicant laid out a plan with her mom about how much her mom would pay, and she chose her schools accordingly. Thus, if she wanted to go to school across the country in California, she would need to come up with the extra money for travel. Another woman made so much money during her summer internship that she relieved her parents of paying for one semester's tuition after they fell into some tough times. It might feel strange to talk with your parents about money if you aren't used to it, but better to put things out there and be honest.

If you don't have outside financial help, then you will need to have an honest conversation with yourself about what you can pay, how you feel about taking out loans, and what other resources you can find. For many applicants, the financial aid package from schools is a big deciding factor. One friend from Harvard actually got Brown and Harvard to have a bidding war over her. Harvard came up with a package that enabled her to go. Another friend based all of her school choices on the tuition costs, a common approach. She wanted to minimize her loans, so she chose relatively inexpensive schools and ended up at University of Virginia. Some of the finest people I know from Harvard were in the ROTC program to pay for school. Same thing at business school; amazing classmates had done ROTC at places like Princeton. It's obviously an enormous commitment, but they gained unparalleled leadership training and maturity.

Of course, you can also explore options for work-study programs. Not all work-study jobs are pushing administrative papers or cleaning dorm bathrooms, though many are. One of my applicants for business school had an undergrad work-study job that ended up being more like a research project. During my one semester of law school, I got approval to have my work-study job become an internship of sorts with the Washington, D.C., Juvenile Justice

Department, because I was interested in that field. I spent every Friday at a prison for young boys in Oak Hill, Maryland, helping them draft letters to their attorneys and seeing a very different world from the Georgetown law classroom.

Finally, there's the option of applying for grants (from the schools and outside sources). One of my applicants worked a massive book of grants to find anything and everything she qualified for based on her background and professional interests. This woman worked it, and she ended up with a few options. There are also programs like the Posse Foundation, which helps students who may be overlooked by the traditional college application process get scholarships. Please talk to your guidance counselor, a teacher, or another adult who can help you out. Let them know if you need help with ideas for finding grants. (We'll talk more about the people on your side in chapter 4.)

Keep in mind that although going into educational debt is an investment that will pay off, it is still debt, and you need to determine for yourself how you feel about that. Money, debt, and loans can all seem like very scary stuff as you become an adult. It's easy to think that if we don't pay attention to it, it will just go away. But like anything a little dark, if you don't shine some light onto it, it only grows bigger and darker. Try to take the money bull by the horns, so to speak, as early in life as possible. Your financial situation is usually a reflection of your inner life: for example, if you are feeling confused and chaotic, your finances can reflect that. So stepping into the process in an informed and honest manner can be a great first step to becoming a financially stable adult.

Here are some questions to consider around financial aid:

+ Are your parents or someone else going to help you pay for college? How much? How do you feel about that?

+ How much of your college bill will you be paying? How do you feel about that?

+ Will you be applying to private or public schools? Is money guiding that decision? How do you feel about that?

+ Will you take on student loans to pay for college? How do you feel about that? Do you understand what that means in terms of paying back the money? How can you get information to understand loans and their obligations?

+ Would you be willing to take on more student loans to go to a more expensive school?

+ Who will be paying for your expenses during college? If it's you, how do you intend to make money for this? Work during the year? During summers?

+ Are you going to do work-study? Do you understand what this means and how it works at your schools of interest?

+ Are you applying for scholarships and grants, either given by your schools or by outside organizations? Where can you learn more about these? What are the deadlines? What information do you need to submit for these?

Courses, Majors, Study Abroad: Making Sure Your College Choices Have the Classes You Want to Take

Oh right, you're going to class, too. Sorry, with all of the talk of friends and weather and sports and clubs and frats and food, it's easy to forget that you're there to hit the books. And please do hit the books! With a nod to the previous section on financial aid, at some point in every college student's life, you do the math on what each hour of class costs. When I went to college, I think every class skipped was $50 down the drain, and I'm sure it's more now. Your parents didn't take out a second mortgage on their house for you to sleep in. You aren't going to your work-study job all afternoon to blow off your papers in the evening. Try to wake up, walk through the snow, turn away from the waves, and go to class.

Now maybe you have known that you wanted to be a doctor (or engineer or flutist) from the time you were six. That's awesome. But for most of us, at 17, we're unsure of what we want to be when we grow up—and for some of us that status remains for, let's just say, a very long time. We'll get into that issue in chapter 2 on following your bliss. (I'm really talking up that chapter, aren't I? I've mentioned it a couple of times already. It's a good time, though. I mean, how can it not be a good time when we're talking about bliss?)

Anyway, some of you who are more certain of your bliss may be sure what you want to study at school. Obviously, you'll be looking for schools with a strong pre-med or engineering or flute program. I know a woman whose son has known from the time he could talk that he loved light. He studied lighting tech at college and now does the lights for major television broadcasts. One guy I worked with on business school applications was thinking about majoring in engineering at University of California–Berkeley starting in eighth grade. However, whether you are sure of your path or not, it pays to do a little thinking on this before you go.

You may have a sense of what courses or majors are important to you or not. Either way, definitely look through colleges' course options and see what you're drawn to. One of my friends drooled over the course catalogues when she was considering schools. Now she's a jaded lawyer and realizes that the schools were just doing a good job of marketing, a position my skeptic dad liked to take when I did the same drooling over the massive Harvard book of courses each year. Marketing or not, let yourself pour over those and start thinking about what you want to study and what schools will let you do that. Even if you think you're clueless about what you want to study, you really aren't. You have a sense of your interests. Let your mind start to run wild with the opportunities ahead.

Maybe you already know that you want to study abroad. Some schools make this easier than others. So many friends (from Georgetown, Holy Cross, Bates, Amherst... the list goes on and on) cited their semesters or years abroad as a highlight of their college experience. One woman had to tussle with the academic studies department at her fancy East Coast school, which will remain nameless though I think they've gotten their act together now, to get credit for her service work in Africa. If you love to travel or you're looking forward to college for the chance to travel, please check into the options. (It's also something to tell schools that you want to do, which we'll hit in chapter 3 on the essays.)

But remember, even if you are sure what you want to study right now, things change. The business school applicant who started thinking in eighth grade about majoring in Engineering at Berkeley? He went to Berkeley, majored in engineering, and changed to economics by junior year. So keep your mind and options open. There are so many possibilities for your life, your academic life in this case, that you can't even begin to imagine. The point for now is to let yourself start thinking about what's pulling you in.

Here are some questions to consider around academic life:

- Do you know what you want to study? Can you do that at this school?
- Do you want to double-major or minor in other areas of interest?
- Do you get excited looking over the course options?
- Are you looking for tons of course options?
- Do you want a structured core curriculum?
- Do you want no core curriculum or loose requirements?
- What is the average course load? Does that seem right for you?

- Do you have any learning disabilities? Contact the school to see how those could be accommodated.
- Do you want preprofessional options? Do you want a liberal arts curriculum?
- Do you want to study abroad? Is that encouraged and/or possible?
- Do you want academic guidance? Is that available?

Do Your Homework: It's about *You* Choosing Them

Doing your homework on schools is a huge part of the choosing. Don't just apply to Wake Forest because the hot girl in calculus says it's a great place. Think for yourself on this one. You can find other ways to impress the hot girl in calculus, like sharing your research on Wake Forest.

None of this stuff on how to research schools is rocket science. If anything, you're up to your ears in it already. What I want to emphasize is that you're doing research to see what *you* think about a school; keep the focus on whether or not *you* want to go there. It's not about applying to where you think it would be cool to be accepted or applying where other people want you to apply. We'll get to more on this in the next section. For starters, let's take a quick look at how to do this research.

When doing homework on colleges, school websites are a great place to start, as are school view books. I hear you—these websites and view books can start to look the same. But they really aren't. If you spend some time with them, you'll get not only information on all of the offerings but also a feel for the culture and values. One applicant found that she wanted to read the view book for Duke over and over again, whereas she gave the one for Colby to a friend. Her instincts were starting to speak out as to where she wanted to be. Plus, from the websites and the view books, you'll get a sense of what you want to join or start, which you can speak to in your essays (more to come on those in chapter 3).

Also, as mentioned, schools often have student representatives you can speak with or email to get more information. They can be a great source on the current state of affairs at a school. Same goes for alumni—the more recent, the better. See if the schools are hosting panel events in your area, even at your high school, with admissions reps and/or alums. These tend to come up more for graduate schools, but undergrads host them as well. Alums, especially those who attend recruiting events, love to gush about their schools. They will give you a good flavor for the place. Remember, though, everything that students and alums say is filtered through their personal experiences. So take it with a grain of salt, meaning know that *your* priorities and interests will define *your* experience.

This brings us to the school visit. Should you visit schools? Sure, if you have the time and money. If you don't, don't worry about it. It's really as simple as that. I think the most important aspect of the school visit is what your gut says about the place (more on that in the next section). How do you feel when you're walking around and talking to current students? Do you want to stay?

In terms of helping your application, school visits do show interest in the school, but admissions committees know that not everyone can get there. They won't hold a lack of a visit against you. While you can use a visit to gather details for your admissions essay about why you're a good fit for the school, you can get that off of the Web, too. While visiting, you may or may not meet admissions staff members. If you do, don't expect them to turn around and write a sticky note saying, "Note to self: Accept that Anna from Skokie no matter what her application looks like. Love her!" Sucking up during your visit doesn't really give you a leg up. So if you can't visit, then don't think about it for another second. Seriously, chill. You can get all the information you need to make a decision and write your essays from the website, view book, and speakers at your school or in your hometown.

If you can only make one visit, save it for the admit weekend. Again, this is because visiting before you apply does not really help your chances of getting in. However, many applicants have told me that a visit during admit weekend helped them make their decisions. During a pre-application school visit, you get a tour and information session with your parents, and they will probably have a better time than you. In contrast, at admit weekend, you'll meet potential future classmates and get a much more in-depth, personalized experience of the school. One applicant was stunned by how much more she loved University of North Carolina during the admit weekend. Another confirmed her growing suspicion that her previously beloved Dartmouth wasn't actually the right place for her. Another friend was certain he was going to Harvard or Yale, but then at the Stanford admit weekend, he just didn't want to leave. Stanford it was. You'll be able to feel what it would be like to be a student there. And following that feeling will tell you whether or not it's the place for you.

But again, you know all this stuff about how to do your research. You're reading a book about applying after all. Let's get into something much juicier—how you make your decisions.

Pay Attention to Your Gut Instincts: Using Intuition

There are so many voices in your head as you make your way through the college application process. As mentioned in the introduction, our minds chatter all the time. They skip about to the past and future, resting anywhere but the present, telling us all kinds of stories about ourselves—what we can and can't do, what we should and shouldn't do. But now you also have the opinions of many outside parties: parents, siblings, friends, boyfriends, girl-friends, classmates, teachers, coaches, guidance counselors, college advisors, admissions consultants, friends of parents, parents of friends, friends of siblings, siblings' friends, bloggers, writers, the checker at the grocery store, whomever. (And some of these are helpful, but some not, which we'll look at in chapter 4.) Everyone is ready to ask you a question and give you a thought on your college applications.

But the only voice that matters is *yours*. And I mean that inner voice, the wisest part of you, the part that already knows the answers. You just have to ask and listen. Your inner voice isn't part of the chattering up in your head. It's the voice that comes from your heart and your gut; it's your intuition. Listening to your intuition is about trusting yourself. It's about feeling your instincts and following them. The less you trust yourself, the more you listen to all of those outside parties and their opinions. The less you trust yourself, the more you give in to the fearful voices inside your busy mind that say you are less than, that you don't deserve more, that you can't do this. As your confidence grows, so too will your capacity to know what is right for you. Let this application process be practice for making decisions for yourself, which is a crucial piece of living a healthy, honest life as an adult.

Listening to our intuition allows us to recognize signs—the proverbial burning bush is around us all the time; we just need to trust ourselves enough to see it. Your busy mind wants to sell you all kinds of stories about the past and future so that you make decisions based on old patterns, fear of failure, or just plain old ego. Save yourself a lot of pain and frustration by listening to your body and heart. Your instincts and intuition—your wiser consciousness—are spread throughout your body. Listening to them means learning to take your head out of the game a bit. So if a college that sounds perfect on paper feels cold and unwelcoming on admit weekend, then it's not the right place for *you*. It's all about how you *feel* in situations; it doesn't matter what you think you're supposed to do or what others say is right (no matter who! even your parents). So rather than braining your way through decisions, start to *feel* your way through.

That's easier said than done, though. We're all very good at thinking. It takes some practice to get good at feeling. Fortunately, you've got all of the equipment you need to start feeling your way through the world: your body! Now things are about to get a little "yoga teacher hoo-hah" as I like to say, but hang with me here. Even my most skeptical friends have come to appreciate that they can be healthier and happier if they recognize feelings in their bodies.

Sometimes what's easier than recognizing feelings in your body is recognizing symptoms your body develops when you *aren't* listening to those feelings. I learned this the hard way by not listening to my instincts for a couple of years. When I ignored my gut — literally — it started talking to me. During my post–Stanford business school years, I began developing a lot of stomach problems. It was a time when I wasn't following my instincts. I won't bore you with the details, but suffice it to say that I stayed way too long in a relationship that made me feel bad about myself and at jobs that made me feel stupid and unmotivated. No offense to the boyfriend or the bosses; I obviously was not feeling good about myself and gave out an energy that said, "Yes, please confirm to me that I'm worthless." After all, we get back what we give out. (It's a karma thing, which we'll discuss more in chapter 5.) Gradually, my stomach started behaving in a completely unfamiliar way, and I was in constant abdominal pain. Even as things ended with the boyfriend and I left the jobs, I was stuck with residual self-doubt and anxiety from having let others chip at my self-worth and not trusting myself to know what was best for me.

Fortunately, I was also getting deeper into yoga, and one aspect of the yoga practice that helped big-time was learning about the energy body, or the chakra system. Before this time, like perhaps many of you, I had imagined that proponents of chakra wisdom danced around with crystals in flowing skirts adorned with feathers. But as I got deeper into yoga, I noticed that the twisting and inverting and stretching helped not only my stomach (and entire body) but also my mind and emotions. Moreover, I started to see the inverse — how much the mind and emotions affect the body.

We're all made up of energy. Currents of energy run through us. You can think of it in a purely scientific way. In yoga philosophy, this energy is called *prana*; it is your life force. Sounds very Star Wars, right? Turns out the Force is, indeed, with you! You may have heard this energy called *chi*, which is the term used in traditional Chinese medicine. Prana or chi or energy runs throughout your body along energy channels, or meridians. And we have a couple of big energy centers running up the core of our bodies; that's what the *chakras* are. But your energy can get stuck in places in your body; you can develop tension, pain, and illness.

As I found more and more through yoga, your body is a reflection of your internal mental and emotional state. You know when you just feel kind of bummed and you look it? And the opposite is true, too: when you feel good, people can tell. Also, you know how you are just drawn to certain people? There's brightness in their eyes and a natural glow to them. It has nothing to do with height, weight, hair, looks, age; they are just attractive. You're attracted to their radiance. They've got good energy. Prana's a flowin'. Niiiiiiice chi.

In my case, I was having stomach and digestion issues at a time when my self-confidence was at an all-time low. I wasn't trusting myself or taking responsibility for my place in the world, and I was letting other people (or really my impression of what other people thought) dictate how I lived my life. Does this sound similar, maybe, to what you're going through now? Trying to decide what you're going to do for the rest of your life, choose a college that's going to help you prepare for that, find a way to pay for it, and find a way to fit in at that school — all while your parents, siblings, teachers, coaches, friends, and friends' parents are probably also weighing in on what *they* think you should do? I was in the same place then: I felt as though I was constantly performing for others, doing what I thought made them happy, instead of doing what felt right for me. So deep down, I had no respect for myself because I wasn't listening to my instincts on who I actually was. I wasn't listening to my *gut*, one of the big time chakras, so my gut rebelled.

What got me back on track was when I followed my instincts about how to live my life — what my work was, whom I hung out with, how I spent my time. I reclaimed a personal sense of power, listened to my body, and started following my gut. Accordingly, my gut (and all of me) became much happier and healthier. And I did it without wearing a feather skirt!

Anyway, let's get back to what *you're* feeling right now — because *you* should be who matters most to you. My point simply is that paying attention to your body can help you can recognize some of the emotional dissonance you may have in your life. For your purposes, when selecting schools and making big decisions, it's worth it to tap into physical cues that help you know what you're feeling, especially in your gut and heart (although your feelings may register in other places in your body as well).

And if you think all this mind-body connection stuff seems irrational and weird, consider: is it more rational to pick schools based on where your summer crush is applying? Don't act like you don't know what I'm talking about!

So bear with me, and let's explore ways to tap into what you are feeling in your body, not thinking in your head. If you're really not into this, you can skip ahead to the end of this chapter where I talk about competition and running your own race, but it might be worth taking a few minutes to help deal with the difficult stuff you're going through right now. I admit that for a lot of us, it's tough to give ourselves over to the airy-fairyness of this idea. But give it a shot: I'm only presenting one exercise that you can do on your own, which involves getting physically quiet and observing your feelings. Then I'll give you a few suggestions on how to pay attention to your energy when you're out in the world experiencing things, talking with people, and dealing with all the external chatter that can get in the way of your making a decision about what's right for *you* in the next four years and after.

Follow the Energy Exercise

Find a place to be alone, someplace quiet — no media, music, phones, email, etc. Put yourself in a comfortable position, whether that's sitting or lying down. (Note: Lying down can be risky because there's a sleepy factor, especially when you're exhausted from balancing school, activities, and college stuff.) If you're sitting, make sure you're comfy and prop yourself up.

Take a couple of breaths. First, just start noticing that you are inhaling and exhaling. Let yourself feel how the inhale lifts and spreads your ribs. Let yourself feel how the exhale chills you out a bit. Gradually, you can deepen your inhales and exhales, imagining the inhales running up the front of your body and the exhales flowing down the back of your body. The inhales naturally lift up your breastbone; the exhales let your shoulder blades slide down your back. Close your eyes and take at least ten long, slow, smooth breaths just like this. Enjoy it.

When you're ready, let whatever it is you're considering come into your mind — a specific school, a part of the country, a social scene you might want, activities to do, or academic areas of interest. Rather than just imagining what it might be like to be there or experience that, try to put yourself there so you can feel it. For example, you *are* captain of the volleyball team at the University of Southern California, or you're *in* the library studying pre-med at the University of Chicago. Be with that experience as much as you can. If it helps, talk to yourself as though you're describing your life in that place to someone. Get into it. You're alone, so don't worry about feeling like a fool. If it helps, go to a mirror and describe your life to the mirror so you can see how you look. Really try to become to that version of yourself.

As you're talking about this life or just being in it, start to notice how your energy feels. Is your chest getting light? Is your abdomen relaxed? Or is there gripping anywhere? Do you want to keep being in this place? Are you excited? Or are you getting tired? Are you bored with this scene? Sitting here embodying yourself in this imagined life, do you want more and more of it? If you're looking in a mirror, do you look excited and energized? Do you want to keep going and make up more details about this life?

When things make you feel good and inspired and excited to be alive, you should follow that energy. Keep breathing deeply into your chest and see how you feel. Register where in your body feelings come up. Excitement doesn't have to manifest in a certain place—maybe it's a fun, fluttery feeling in your stomach, maybe your heart feels open, maybe you tingle through your fingers and toes, or maybe you feel really still and peaceful. It's your body; learn to read it.

Follow the Energy into the Wild World at Large

You can also pay attention to your energy when you're out and about in the world. Let's take the most obvious example. When you are visiting a school, how do you feel there? It's totally legit to ask, "Can I see myself here?" But that can get a little cerebral. So try to just notice if you want to be there.

For example, when I was deciding between business schools, I went to the admit weekends for Stanford and Harvard. At Stanford's weekend, I didn't want to leave: I was ready to move right in and start life there. It just felt great. However, within 15 minutes of the first event at the Harvard weekend, I was ready to leave—which surprised me, because I'd *loved* Harvard undergrad. Don't get me wrong. The people I met at the Harvard Business School admit weekend were great; in fact, they were many of the same folks from the Stanford weekend. I somehow just knew that HBS was a no-go for me. It felt off.

And I had felt that way back in the spring of my senior year of high school when I went to Northwestern's admit weekend. I was ready to leave as soon as I got there, as if someone were saying *no* inside my head. It's just that I didn't know what else to do at the time. Not go to college that year? Beg Tufts to take me off the wait list? But I hadn't felt super psyched when I visited there, either. I felt as though I had no options, so I went to Northwestern. Don't give in to that feeling; you *always* have options (which we'll discuss in chapter 6).

For now, though, try to pay attention to your energy while you're still investigating schools. Let's say you can't do a school visit. You will still get gut feelings when meeting alumni or students or even looking at the website. You know when you have a book that you can't put down? The view books and websites for the schools might feel like that for you. Or when you're talking to people about schools, you'll be able to rattle on and on about schools you feel good about, while you might get a little bored talking about the others. Just keep checking in to see if you're getting good energy from yourself or just nervous energy from feeling like you have to apply someplace to please others. Keep going back to getting still and seeing what you truly feel.

Maybe you can even get specific as to where in your body you feel things. Is there lightness or heaviness in your heart? Is your stomach relaxed or churning? Is it easy to talk about your future plans, or are you getting tension in your neck? Does your appetite seem regular, or are you eating more or less? Can you fall asleep at night, or are you tossing and turning? What is your body saying to you? Overall, you want energy that makes you feel good and confident, not energy that makes you feel nervous and anxious.

Sometimes, you know right away if something is right for you or not. But sometimes, you don't have a clear sense or feeling. When things aren't clear, it's best to give a decision some space before you pull the trigger one way or another. This is the Taoist notion of "action through inaction." Do by not doing. Wait and see. Try to get quiet and let the question just sit with you. Plant the seed of it in your brain before you go to sleep. Ask that wise part of you to consider it as you make your way through the day, and then don't let your chatter mind chew too much. Pay attention to your feelings, wait for signs, write about it in a journal, and see where you go. (We'll talk more about these strategies in chapter 5 on dealing with obstacles.) Let yourself rest in a state of indecision and wait to feel what your body's telling you to do. Remember, the body doesn't lie!

When You're Stuck, Flip a Coin

This next approach to dealing with decisions is a little less hoo-hah. It's a coin toss, but a special one. A professor at business school taught me this, and I'll admit that I've used it quite a bit since then for myself and for friends and applicants. Let's say you're deciding between applying to Washington University or not. Break out your quarter. Assign each side of the coin to the yes and no of your question. Heads would be "I'm applying to Wash U," and tails would be "I'm not applying to Wash U." Then flip your coin. See what the answer is. Pause. Do you want to flip it again? Deep down, you know you have an answer. If you want to stick with what the coin gave you, that's your answer. If you want to flip again, then it's the other option.

All of these practices are just tools to help you connect with the wisdom of your intuition. More and more as you let yourself be open to this idea, you'll notice your energy in different situations, and it will become easier and easier to read what your body is telling you. You were born with these tools. It's not a matter of learning; it's more about uncovering. It about stilling the mind, being present, and being open to what's true for you.

Run Your Own Race

Speaking of your truth, let's visit the idea that this process is about you living *your* life. While it's very human to compare ourselves to others, nothing screws you up more in life than trying to be someone else. And why would you want to be anyone other than you? You rock.

The college application process, and your whole life, is about doing your own practice, running your own race. You have a purpose here that is uniquely yours. Trying to be someone else is a waste of your precious time. Going for goals that come from competition rather than your heart will leave you empty and dissatisfied. You know that feeling, when you've put effort into something because someone told you to: even if you achieve it, you could care less about it. Yet when something comes from your heart, it's a delicious endeavor. Trying to act like or be someone else or achieve their dreams shuts away your Self, the authentic and biggest you. Yet the ego is powerful, and it requires constant vigilance to check that you're moving from the bold desires of your genuine heart, not the petty desires of your human, competitive mind. You can only play your life big if you're playing at *your* life.

I know this is difficult, as everyone around you starts amassing lists of schools. You have to keep asking yourself if you really want to go to Princeton because it feels right to you or because everyone else is applying there. Let yourself get quiet and explore whether you actually want to live at that school for four years. Is that where you want to grow into an adult? Do you feel energetic thinking about that place? Otherwise, applying is a huge waste of your time and money; it's also a waste of your efforts and attention, which could be focused on schools that are actually a good fit for unique you.

Check Out Your Feelings around Competition

The ego also has a festival around competing with your classmates and even friends over grades and SATs. Quieting the comparing mind gets very difficult when things like class rank come out. First, it feels disgusting to be reduced to a number in any situation. Plus, the competition aspect of class rank is so blatant that it's almost absurd. For example, my friends and I took the ironic approach and called each other by our numbers for a day (47, 113, 25). It was funny until one friend revealed she was 2; then the rest us got annoyed. The SATs are even more ridiculous: talk about being reduced to a number! One thing that might illuminate how much your SATs don't matter down the line is that everyone I ask can't remember his or her score. But there's so much ranking and scoring at this time in your life—which makes your ego soooo excited to get in there and compare yourself over and over again.

For some people, there's a charge around this competition. Maybe it excites you, probably because you've been on top. For others, competing is a huge energy drain, a depressing feeling. It's worthwhile to look at your reaction; both are very human. That said, both are going to bring you suffering eventually if you don't let go of that comparing mind.

You can get really into the competition, but someone is always going to be better than you at something, sometime. Oddly enough, I felt really grateful at Harvard that I hadn't been the best academically at my high school. Most people there had been academic all-stars, and it was tough for them not to be the best at Harvard. So if you're really into being better than everyone else, this is a good time to explore where that's coming from and try to look at what it would be like to do for the sake of doing—to do for the sake of being more yourself rather than better than someone else.

The flip side is feeling that you can never be as good as the others. It's a great time to check out that, too. As good as the others at what? Calculus? Getting into Columbia? Try shifting the definition of success into *how* you do things, not *what* you do. That's sort of the varsity level of living life from a higher mind. It's interesting, though. Could you put the emphasis on how you behave in situations rather than the outcomes? Did you handle your calculus struggle with dignity and patience? There's also the karmic idea that maybe there are really important lessons you're supposed to be learning by struggling with calculus. Maybe working your tail off to get that B was how you learned how to stick with a challenge and be compassionate towards yourself? That's worth much more down the line than breezing through without noticing and getting an A.

As tough as it is to study our darker emotions this way, this process is a great opportunity to explore your feelings around competition. Know that it's human to feel petty, jealous, and sad about this aspect of the college process. Also know that you're more than that. You'll slip right into your bigger person suit if you let yourself acknowledge the smaller sides of your mind. What you resist persists. So if you keep saying that none of this bothers you (and it actually does), then it's only going to get bigger and more bothersome. If you keep saying that you're not into the competition (but you really are), you're just going to get more and more sucked into feeling that you always have to be the best. And the competition thing just goes on and on and on through your adult life with jobs, grad schools, salaries, where *your* kids go to college... it's endless. You will save yourself a world of suffering if you start training yourself to shift perspective and be grateful for where you are and what you have going on right now. Let success be who you are rather than what you do.

Also, the good news is that schools are higher minded than you might believe. They would love to see a more complete picture of you than your grades, but you have to show it to them. This means that if you have a low GPA or some issue with your grades, you need to tell them the story behind it. (More to follow on this in chapter 3 on the essay.) For now, the general point is that if you are truly learning for the sake of learning and exploring interests and unfolding lessons about yourself, then you're on the right track. Demonstrating self-awareness around your learning process and your "successes and failures" is a hallmark of maturity. I have had countless applicants who struggled with grades at some point, and some of their best essays were about this challenge. That low-GPA essay ended up being a revealing story about battling with depression, helping a sick parent, or just being immature. And those students needed to show schools the lessons they learned from their situations. You can prevent schools from seeing you as merely a number. You just need to see yourself that way first.

Ultimately, this process is really a beautiful opportunity to cultivate a spirit of noncompetition and rise to a place of compassion and celebration. A first step could be not participating in the inevitable gossip about classmates and friends and their SATs, grades, school choices, etc.

The one school tour I remember during my junior year spring break college tour bonanza with my parents is Harvard. But out of high school, I certainly wasn't applying there! I didn't have the grades, scores, activities, or anything to compete on that level (I thought). Besides, at the time, Harvard seemed scary, reserved for kids who were more intense than I was, not the welcoming, fun home I found later. But back during junior year, my parents and I went simply as sightseers because I was looking at Tufts. Upon arriving at the tour, I saw two kids from my high school. We were all in choir and honors classes together, but they got better grades than I did. I walked over with my parents to say hi, but I was a little embarrassed. I didn't want my classmates to think that I thought I could compete on this level. My worst fear was realized when the girl said, "*You're* applying to Harvard???" My parents were a little taken aback at her attitude, and my mom's heart visibly broke for me. I tried to play it off, smiling as I told the girl that we were just taking the tour because it was so pretty and then assuring my parents as we walked away that I didn't care. But I could not have felt dumber.

I recently told this story to an applicant, who said, "Oh my God, that's so *Mean Girls*!" Totally! In fact, there's much wisdom, for all ages, in one of the final moments of *Mean Girls* when the main character realizes that

> Calling somebody else fat
>   won't make you any skinnier.
> Calling someone stupid
>   doesn't make you any smarter.

In the same vein, gossiping about someone's low SAT score doesn't make yours any higher. Criticizing someone else's academic and extracurricular profile doesn't make yours any stronger. Mocking someone on your college tour doesn't improve your chances of getting in.

Can you use the experience of applying alongside friends and classmates to practice not comparing yourself to others when it comes to college stuff and maybe other things as well? Maybe you can take it to another level and practice being supportive instead? Remember, what you put out comes back to you. If you want support and affirmation, then give it. What would it feel like to be compassionate when your peers struggle and joyful when they succeed? Probably great. And perhaps they will shine that light right back on you. Cultivating this perspective is a discipline. Sometimes, you have to fake it till you make it. But it will feel so good that it will become part of your nature. And you can become a shining example to the rest of us.

✦ ✦ ✦

Speaking of being a shining example, it's time to talk about how to shine in the eyes of colleges. Since we've done some thinking about how to consider schools, in chapter 2, we'll explore how to make yourself more appealing as an applicant. You might be pleasantly surprised!

CHAPTER 2

❖

What Can I Do to Be More Attractive to Schools?

Follow Your Bliss

The single most frequent question I hear from applicants is "What can I do to be more attractive to schools?" Every student wants specific answers on what extracurriculars to do, what jobs to take, which classes to pursue. The answer is simple, but it can be frustrating. *Do what genuinely inspires you*, I tell them. *Follow your bliss.*

How annoying is that advice? Each applicant's immediate irritation with me is almost palpable. "Look, lady, I'm stressing out over grades, essays, tests, jobs, extracurriculars … and now I'm supposed to follow my freaking bliss? What does that even mean?

Skipping through a field of daisies, wearing a flowing robe, and playing a lute while angels sing overhead? And when exactly will I find the time for the skipping and the lute playing when I have all of this stuff to get done *right now?* Can you ditch that hippie-dippie yoga vibe for a moment and call on your practical MBA brain to give me some advice that I can actually use?"

Alas, I cannot ditch my hippie-dippie yoga side (encouraging you to follow your bliss is *my* bliss—sorry!). Don't worry, though, my MBA brain is always on, and in this chapter, we'll look at how following your bliss during your college application process is both soulful and savvy. Following your bliss is all about being real, and the good news is that colleges *also* want you to be real. They are not interested in some carefully manufactured persona of who you think they want you to be. Seriously. Colleges are not looking to have a bunch of burned-out freshman who have been jumping through hoops for the past four years trying to be artistic, ath-letic, scientific, poetic, philanthropic, and oh-so-perfectly perfect. The admissions committees are looking to create a well-rounded class, where each student brings genuine, unique contributions to the college's complex, interesting, diverse scene. This means that instead of trying to be perfect on paper, you can work on being *perfectly you.* What a relief!

Being you is no small task, though. Deep down, you know what makes you feel just like you. But it requires some vigilance to stay true to yourself, because outside pressures and influences and internal mind chatter block that. So in this chapter, we're going to look a bit more at what bliss is (being you!) and how it feels when you tap into it. Then we'll explore three things you already have that can help you follow your bliss: gifts, values, and callings. The goal is for you to walk away with a grounded, real-world sense of what extracurricular, academic, and maybe even professional pursuits make you feel real and alive, uplifted, and oh-so-effortlessly you. Break out your flowing robe and cue the lutes!

So What Is "Bliss"? And How Is It Going to Help Me Get into College?

Let's start with a little break-it-down on bliss. The phrase "follow your bliss" was coined by Joseph Campbell, a writer and professor of mythology and religion. He taught at Sarah Lawrence for almost 40 years and was a big influence on George Lucas in the creation of the *Star Wars*. It seems that bliss is being genuine in your work and play and relationships. As Campbell (1991, 15) said, "The privilege of a lifetime is being who you are." In simple terms, bliss is a deep sustained, peace that comes from being yourself.

One important disclaimer to start with: following your bliss does not mean that you are happy, happy and full of joy, joy all the time. These days, we are very caught up in the pursuit of happiness—a totally worthy goal, especially compared to the pursuit of greed, envy, or ego! Books are popping up all over about finding happiness, and Harvard even offers a course on it. Seems that we all need some help in this department, because our culture tends to equate happiness with getting what you want. Whether it's a shirt or a car or a grade or a girl or a guy or a college or a job, we are tempted by the sparkly façade of that thing we have to have. We seek out the thrill of the chase, the excitement of getting… something!

But looking for things outside of you to bring you happiness is actually a royal downer (I'll talk more about this in chapter 6). That new car or new guy may give you momentary excitement, but none of it will deliver sustained happiness. The car breaks down, and you're bummed. Or the car is fine, and you just kind of lose the thrill. The guy ends up being a jerk, and you're weepy. Or the guy is cool, but eventually you go to different colleges and there's some heartbreak. You see, when you rely on stuff or people to keep you happy, you end up in a world of hurt because none of these things last. This is not meant to be depressing—instead it's liberating! You don't have to forgo all of life's earthly pleasures or love-filled relationships to find happiness. Just don't expect them to bring you sustained contentment. Don't expect them to bring you bliss. That's up to you to do solo.

Wait, though, what about worthwhile goals, like searching for not-stuff-induced-happiness or getting into college? Won't reaching those bring some bliss? Not necessarily: as I found out after getting into Harvard, one of the best aspects of achieving a seemingly big-deal thing is seeing that it *doesn't* make you happy forever after. If anything, achieving that type of goal often makes you feel a little guilty for *not* feeling happy all the time. Those days when I walked through campus stressing about some paper or bummed out about some boy, I'd catch myself: "Get a grip, girlfriend. You're at Harvard. Stop whining."

But it's unrealistic to be happy all the time. That's the ironic bit about the whole pursuit-of-happiness thing. Happiness, as we tend of think of it, is an emotion, and emotions come and go. Attaching to emotions is just as painful as attaching to things or people, because emotions are also impermanent. The thrill of getting into Elon or Emory will fade, as will the agony of being rejected from Dickinson or Davidson. After the thrill of victory or the agony of defeat goes, you are still *you*. Think about it for a second. Remember the last time something really tough happened to you? Or something really wonderful? That feeling didn't last forever, did it? You certainly felt the emotions, and that's great. Feeling stuff is key to being a living, compassionate human! So don't ignore the good or repress the bad. Quite the contrary, feel it all in the moment: feel the joy, feel the pain. Then be willing to let it all go — and experience whatever comes next.

The point is that if getting into college isn't going to bring you sustained happiness, then for sure you are not going to find happiness in busting your tail to do a bunch of stuff just for the sake of getting into college. All of that tail busting will probably just bring you stress. Like Pig Pen with his dust cloud, you'll get an anxiety swirl over your head as you attempt to balance being the captain of the lacrosse team, vice president of Amnesty International, part of the cast of *Fiddler on the Roof,* and a top-scoring mathlete... all the while wondering if it's in vain: will any of those things get me into MIT? Maybe. Maybe not. And even if you get in to MIT, you may or may not decide to *go* to MIT. There are never any guarantees. Your dream school may not want you. Or, come springtime, you may not want your dream school. Stranger things have happened. I've seen people turn down Stanford, UPenn, Harvard…just because they changed their minds. You might, too. So if you're just doing things for the end result, you're signing up for many tiresome days of going through the motions, as well as many sleepless nights wondering about the future, a future that won't even happen as you're imagining it. It's a huge waste of your precious time and energy to churn up the Pig Pen anxiety swirl.

The other approach is to do things now that you love to do because you love to do them. Now we are onto the search for bliss! Exciting as it is, following your bliss is actually a quiet, introspective task, because you are looking for sustainable contentment.

This doesn't mean you aren't looking for happiness. Quite the contrary. In fact, you are going to use your heart and gut to discover when you feel truly happy. Once you begin to recognize what that deep happiness feels like, then you can put more of those moments into your life. You will still have highs and lows, because that's life, but you will rest in knowing that you are on your path. Yes, your unique path.

For example, when I was at Northwestern, my favorite class was my freshman seminar on women writers. It was the first time I had read things like *A Room of One's Own*, and something in me stirred. Once I dropped out, I considered transferring to schools with a full women's studies major. So while I was living at home in Maryland and looking for more to do than waiting tables, I interned at the National Organization for Women

(NOW). Feminism wasn't ever discussed in my house growing up, and I was a little intimidated by the hard-coreness of the women at NOW. But I loved it there and worked on their programs for young women. Once at Harvard, I thrived in my women's studies major, focusing on policy and literature, especially African-American women's fiction. It felt so indulgent to study only stuff I loved. I'll never forget the week when I was reading *Beloved* by Toni Morrison for three classes at the same time—heaven! I wrote my senior thesis on the program for teenage moms at the local public high school, and spending time with those incredible young women was a big part of my inspiration to apply for Teach For America. When I followed my interests in a genuine way, I was deeply content in my courses and professional life. My path felt right on.

But hang on here. With that example, I'm feeding your achievement-oriented mind, which thinks that following your bliss is an accomplishment or something that you're supposed to produce. Calm down. Remember: Success in this model isn't *what* you do but *how* you do it. Bliss isn't something you write/make/sell/start and then cross off a to-do list. Rather, following your bliss is constantly listening to your heart about who you are and letting that shine out into every moment of your living. It is about revealing your Self, the you that transcends your active body and busy mind. Again, this is your *deepest you*, the *knowing you*, even the *divine within you*. So to take it up a notch, following your bliss may be the very reason why you are here on earth. For real. There is something in each moment that you bring to this world that is completely different from what anyone else brings. As Martha Graham, a pioneer in modern dance, put it to Agnes de Mille (1991, 264), "There is a vitality, a life force, an energy, a quickening, that is translated through you into action, and because there is only one of you in all time, this expression is unique." You're uniquely fabulous, and we'd all love to see it. In fact, we're all counting on you to bring it—and I mean bring it! Your bliss is the contribution that only you can bring to this world.

You may produce big things (by earthly standards) by following your bliss ... or you may not. Moreover, you may not even know the ripple effects of following your bliss, the lives you touch, the events you influence. Although it's hard to do, it helps to release that immediate gratification framework because, as we know, the earthly stuff comes and goes. Instead, the goal here is to be genuinely you all the time, because being you begets bliss.

Of course, being you is both the easiest and the hardest thing in the world. In addition to the ego- and fear-based voices in your mind about what you're supposed to be and do, you take in a zillion messages from outside sources—parents, siblings, friends, teachers, media, coworkers, teammates, organizations, people you haven't seen since elementary school, people you walk by on the street. It's like a constant Greek chorus running through your brain. Often, these sources aren't even intending to give you messages. Also, keep in mind that *you* are part of the Greek chorus for a zillion *other* people, whether you're trying to be or not. All of us, as fearful, approval-seeking humans, add the Greek chorus to our mind chatter, until we're swimming in opinions on our behavior, actions, goals, college choices, extracurriculars, jobs, boyfriends, girlfriends, car, clothes, hair, diet, you name it.

So how do you find that sense of self to reveal your real Self? This goes back to the idea of feeling your way through life, calling on your knowing mind as opposed to letting the your thinking mind run the show. It's about listening to that intuition coming from your heart and gut (which we discussed in chapter 1) so you can feel when you're genuine and alive. It's recognizing those moments of flow so you can follow your energy. Maybe you already recognize that feeling; maybe you don't. To help you figure that out, we'll move now to the real-life business of getting into your gifts. Gifts are the big clue in recognizing and feeling that unique expression of you so you can get on the road to bliss.

Gifts: You've Got Them, so Share Them with the World (and Colleges)

Your gifts are the talents that you won in the life lottery. You were born with them, and they are just waiting to bust out. For some, these gifts seem obvious. Maybe you knew a kid in second grade who could play Beethoven piano sonatas, while you killed time on a xylophone and waited for recess. Or maybe you watched friends pick up geometry effortlessly, while you wished you were home playing a Beethoven piano sonata. Or maybe you are wondering if you've missed your gifts entirely because you didn't focus a little more on that xylophone.

Don't worry, if the xylophone didn't jump out at you, it wasn't your gift. Your gifts are the things that come *effortlessly* to you—the activities and topics that draw you in. For instance, I have a seven-year-old nephew who has a natural gift for mechanics and engineering. A lot of little boys go through a construction-loving phase; it seems to come just after trains and right before dinosaurs. But my nephew stayed right there: he cannot get enough of thinking about how to build vehicles or space ships or anything. My brother, in an effort to promote well-roundedness in his son, signs him up for basketball, art, whatever. My nephew digs art class, especially if he can build something. But at basketball, he is painfully bored. My brother has to bribe him to try his best at basketball practice. But the reward my nephew wants for good basketball effort… is to describe how to build vehicles during the car ride home. He's clearly creating the next generation of hybrids!

Spending time with kids can be a great way to remind yourself of what bliss and flow feel like. Little kids courageously and shamelessly follow their energy to do what they love. When my nephew is talking about machines or science, he's on fire. I get a charge just being in his presence. As we grow up, we get trained to cooperate and do things that bore us, and a certain degree of that is necessary to participate in civilized society. That said, as we get older, a lot of us forget what it's like to feel so excited just doing things we love.

A great description of how it feels to be in the flow and how following your bliss reveals the Self comes from *The Art of Learning* by Josh Waitzkin, who was this incredible chess prodigy. He'd sit in Washington Square Park in New York's Greenwich Village as a little kid and whomp all the old chess masters. He was the subject of the book and movie *Searching for Bobby Fisher*. He wrote (2007, xii), "Since childhood, I had treasured the sublime study of chess, the swim through ever-deepening layers of complexity. I could spend hours at a chessboard and stand up from the experience on fire with insight about chess, basketball, the ocean, psychology, love, art. The game was exhilarating and also spiritually calming. It centered me. Chess was my friend."

How awesome is that? It's about so much more than just chess. When he is playing, everything feels connected and makes sense; he's at one with the world and himself in a state of deep peace.

Now what about you? Well, there is something, and probably more than one thing, that makes *you* feel like that. We all have skills and interests that bubble up to the surface. You weren't skipped in the doling out of natural gifts. However, your gifts only grow in direct proportion to how much they are acknowledged. Like giving water and sun to a seed, receiving acknowledgment and support helps your gifts grow.

Unfortunately, many people — and maybe you're one of them — don't have others celebrating their gifts as they grow up … especially if their gifts aren't sitting silently in class and doing well on standardized tests. Even worse, as you get older, your gifts can be squashed down if you think they aren't the right things you should be doing. (Enter the imagined judgmental Greek chorus in your head.) Down the line, you start to feel bored, restless, and defeated on academic paths or in jobs that don't align with your gifts.

But here, on the brink of college, is a key time to reclaim that fire and bring out your gifts. College admissions officers would much rather read about one passion that lights you on fire than a list of activities that look good on paper but don't give you a spark. I promise you that they can tell, from your writing, if you really feel passionate about something. It comes right through on paper—and it definitely comes through in your interviews.

I remember from my days as director of admissions at Teach For America reading essays and talking to applicants about community service projects they just didn't care about but felt would be the "right" preparation for working for us. It was much more appealing to read about and discuss someone's passion for baseball and his subsequent leadership on the baseball team. That is a person who will take charge of something he loves; so if he's enthusiastic about teaching, he'll be on fire in a classroom, totally committed to his students' well-being and achievement. Same thing with colleges. They want you to show up and make an impact on campus by leading in the classes and extracurriculars that you love. So figuring out what gives you that spark is going to make you happier now and far more appealing to schools. The bliss search is a win-win; you're following your heart and becoming a better applicant because of it.

But what if you haven't been able to recognize or pursue something that gives you this spark? I bet you actually know it or have some idea, even if you haven't gone full throttle on it yet. We'll address this a bit more in chapter 3 on the essays, but you can introduce your passions elsewhere on your application by telling schools what you hope to pursue at college.

For example, I had one applicant with excellent grades and a great high school high-jumping career. She could easily have been recruited to jump at a bunch of schools, and that skill alone could have helped her admissions chances. However, when we talked about this path, there was a flatness to the conversation: she actually said, "I'll jump if I have to," in the most dispirited tone I'd ever heard. Ugh. You don't want to go off to college feeling as though you're in high-jumping indentured servitude. Moreover, no admissions officer wants to accept someone who feels like that, and again, you can't hide those emotions in essays and interviews. The admissions committee will feel the flatness and lack of interest.

Then she talked about what she wanted to do instead of jumping at college, which was return to her first love of dance. Her mom had made her stop dancing early in high school because it wasn't going to "get her anywhere" for college. (And before you boo her mom, she had her daughter's best interests at heart and wanted her daughter to have more opportunities than she had, which is totally legit.) Anyway, this girl was looking forward to college as a chance either to minor in dance or pursue it at a serious extracurricular level. So she used her essays as a way to talk about her early love of dance and how she wanted to explore that passion at college, with specific ideas on how she would do that. Even though she was less accomplished in dance than high-jumping, she had shown she could achieve and that she wanted to put her dedication into dance.

Also, your bliss doesn't have to be some organized activity where you wear matching jerseys with 20 other people. Maybe what you love to do isn't conducive to such organization, or maybe you just haven't had the chance to get involved in this way. Maybe you feel most *you* when you're trying a new recipe for chili, sitting silently on the banks of a river, or getting lost in the pages of Russian literature. There are ways that you can dig deeper into anything at college, either on your own or by involving others. Schools are curious about how you'll contribute to the class. So tell them! Maybe you want to write restaurant reviews for the newspaper. Maybe you want to start an outdoor meditation club. Maybe you'll be the dude in the dorm ready to break down Dostoyevsky while your roommate offers back massages. (Note to guys: please try not to be *that* guy offering back massages in your freshman dorm. Chicks do not dig him.)

Some of the most interesting and accomplished people I met in college were not leading some organized college activity. There were these great twin brothers at Harvard who were champion whitewater kayakers. We never saw them kayak because it wasn't a team sport at school and the Charles River isn't exactly whitewater. Yet we all loved listening to their tales of intense training and competition as we hung out in the dining hall enjoying our Chili Con Carne without Meat. And, I'm not gonna lie, the eye candy of their massively developed kayaking pipes was also a draw, but it was mostly just fun and fascinating to learn about the competitive kayaking subculture. Remember when we talked about the importance of soaking up the diversity of college last chapter? This goes for diversity of interests, too. What will *you* offer up to your classmates? More important, how will that school environment help you reveal your Self?

Again, this is not about courting the schools. We're talking about you living your life to the fullest. College is the perfect time to discover and cultivate your bliss, because you will be a happier camper for all your years to come if that bliss finds its way into your professional life. One of the students I mentor through a nonprofit lacked a love of book learning and considered not even applying to college. His passion was running a theater program—writing and directing original pieces that made political statements. The idea of college only became interesting to him when he realized he could study just what he wanted there, theater and politics. He looked specifically at schools where he could nurture these interests, like Yale and the New School. He's fired up now that he can make a career out of his passions.

On that note, when working with graduate school applicants, I hear stories all the time from blissed-out folks about how their childhood loves developed into careers. I've met engineers who, like my nephew, were trying to build cities with Tinkertoys or were dreaming up new machines. One of them is way bitter that he didn't pursue his idea of the remote car lock before the big manufacturers; unfortunately, he was only eight years old when he came up with it. Similarly, the entrepreneurs were always trying to start businesses, like by buying basketball cards low and selling them high. The future pre-meds wanted to bandage everything from stuffed animals to annoyed siblings. The teachers wanted to tell everyone what to do and how to do it (guilty as charged myself!). The psych majors listened to their friends' problems. One finance major I helped with business school applications had his own investment newsletter by age ten. No joke. He developed some genius investment strategy and actually gave lectures to corporate CEOs. Hard-core, but that was for sure his bliss.

Stick with me for just a moment longer as we delve into some postcollege career advice, because this is a very important life happiness point and you can start thinking about it right now. Okay, here's the news flash: work does not have to feel like work. In fact, work can feel like play if you've really gotten to your bliss.

Quick example from my consulting days after business school. Even though I was committed to following my bliss in college and during my work with Teach For America, I lost my way after business school. It seemed time to grow up and take a "real" job, whatever that means, and I had some serious loans to pay back. So I went into consulting. Then four months into my days as a strategy consultant, I had a big Aha! moment. The staffing woman was offering me three projects: a cost-cutting case for a cosmetics company, a staffing redesign for a credit card company, or an operations overhaul for a pharmaceutical company. Although I had the technical skills to do any of these, the thought of actually doing the work made me want to run to the bathroom and weep into my sweater set, which incidentally is what I had been doing with the majority of my time there thus far. I asked her if other people were *ever* excited about the cases she offered up. She said most were always excited. Huh?

I'd assumed everyone forced themselves to go to work there every day. Nope, just me.

Now, for my consulting friends who loved the analytical rigor and problem solving of that job, the thought of writing a book or teaching a room full of people how to do a headstand would probably make them want to run to the bathroom and cry. But for me, those things don't even feel like work. Fortunately, I realized I could either spend my time trudging along as a consultant, or I could flow through my days as a writer and yoga teacher. Turns out that if you're blissed out, then you're far better at your work. If you can channel your natural gifts into your job, then work truly does feel like play. You put your all into it, all the time.

My point in telling you this story about my own postcollege life is that it also applies to your precollege life, because I learned (a little late) that work shouldn't be miserable. As you enter into college, you can start thinking expansively about how your natural gifts can be channeled into a career, rather than following the crowd to jobs that are obvious. One friend from high school considered becoming an opera singer but then decided during college that she didn't have the chops to sing professionally. She ended up going into market research and was bored out of her mind. Recently, she told me she wished she'd considered working for an opera company, staying near her love but maybe not as the talent. In fact, she begged me to give you that example so that you could think broadly at your age about paying attention to what inspires you and finding ways to work in that world.

And, more important, please recognize that *you don't have to be good at everything.* This point may seem obvious, but it's worth stating in our perfectionist, overachiever world: we're all supposed to be good at different things. That's how the world keeps spinning. Moreover, you don't have to enjoy everything you're good at. Just because you're good at something doesn't mean it has to be your bliss. Go back to the student who excels at high-jumping but isn't into it, but she loves to dance. I'm sure there's another girl out there who feels as though she is touching heaven when she high-jumps, so *she* should be the one jumping at school. My student can get her groove on instead. As the 13th-century Persian poet Rūmī (1995, ch. 4) wrote, "Let the beauty we love be what we do. There are hundreds of ways to kneel and kiss the ground." Each of us has a distinct inner light, soul, Self—and this includes *you.* What is *your* Self's unique offering to the world?

✦ ✦ ✦

What's ironic is that it's the *effortless* aspect of our gifts that often makes us miss them. We think that the things that come easily to us come easily to everyone else, too. For example, I worked with an applicant who had no idea what to say at first when I asked her about times in her life when everything felt really easy and good to her. Earlier in our work, she had mentioned her success in leading a charity project. When I asked about that, she said that was easy for her, so it didn't count.

Actually, that's the stuff that counts the *most.* When I pointed out to her that not everyone was successful in raising tons of money and creating a well-attended event, it meant that her gifts in communication, organization, and influence were exceptional and *not* something everyone could do. Her gifts were obvious to her peers, who praised her for her impact, but they weren't obvious to her. After considering this, she began to think very differently about herself as a leader. She thought about what she wanted to lead at school and how she could impact her campus and, down the line, the world!

One of the most important professional and personal steps you can take — whether you are 8, 18, or 58 years old — is to spend some time uncovering your gifts. In fact, if you picked up this book thinking you wanted to be pre-med and, after reading this chapter, you decide you should pursue sociology, then this book was money well spent already. If you picked up this book because you were going to apply to college and have now decided to become a rock star, this money was even better spent, and you can put this book down and go rock on. (I'll deal with the angry emails from your parents.) Maybe you'll go to college after your career on the stage, like so many people I meet in New York. Really, though, as someone who spent too much precious time crying in the bathroom of jobs that were a bad fit, I beg of you to consider your gifts *before* you go to college so you can celebrate and nurture them in this rich time of exploring classes, clubs, and internships... and then have the courage to put them to work in the world.

How to Recognize Your Natural Talents: A Gifts Discovery Exercise

The trick, of course, is discovering your gifts. Again, it's difficult for many of us to shout our gifts out from the rooftops. One big sign of gifts is what you liked to do when you were little, like between the ages of 4 and 14, before the Greek chorus started influencing your decisions. So here are some questions to get you thinking back to those years:

- What were your favorite afterschool activities?
- What were you doing when you lost track of time as a kid?
- What did your parents/teachers have to drag you away from?
- What kinds of books did you like to read?
- What did you get special recognition for?

In addition, I hope you've cultivated some of these gifts, or maybe you've even developed new ones, so here are a few more things to think about:

- What are your favorite things to do these days?
- What are you doing when you lose track of time now?
- What do you have to drag yourself away from to do work?
- What kinds of books do you like to read?
- What do you get praised for?

Sometimes, it's easier to think about how others would describe you, so let's put that Greek chorus to work for you. Take a moment and think about teachers, parents, friends, teammates, and colleagues. How would each of these people describe you? What would they say are your best qualities and your talents? You don't have to ask these people to describe you (although you can do that, too, if you want to); instead, just think—honestly—about what they would say about what you are most gifted, talented, or skilled at.

- Parents
- Teachers
- Siblings
- Friends
- Peers (colleagues at work, teammates, etc.)
- Coaches
- Bosses
- Others?

Finally, consider less traditional things that come easily for you or that you're known for. Don't assume that these things are easy for everyone. What jumps out?

- Your heart, intellect, humor, creativity, passion?
  - One applicant recognized his bliss as stand-up comedy.

- Your love of travel and adventure?
  - Countless applicants apply to schools that prioritize study abroad and write about specific places they want to visit.
- Your ability to solve problems and lead a group?
  - There's a reason why people put you in charge. How can you use this gift to change the world?
- Your ability to throw an awesome dinner party?
  - Think you can't build a life based on this gift? Ask Martha Stewart about it.
- Your resilience?
  - Been through tough things? How does that experience inspire you to help others?
- Watching and discussing movies?
  - Maybe you want to make them?
- Working out?
  - The world needs you to inspire them to be fit, too. How can you share that?
- Having great style? Designing clothes?
  - Find the schools where you can learn how to make it work on the world stage.
- Painting?
  - Please, please find schools where you can nurture this, at the very least as a serious hobby.

* Singing?
    ◦ Ditto above and get ready to sing your tail off at college with a capella groups or bands or at open mic nights.

Think beyond the traditional stuff and really consider what comes easily for you. Then make a list of these attributes and activities.

Putting your gifts into play is the first major step in following your bliss. In this time of self-discovery as you apply to schools, look at whether the type of major or school you're exploring will help you nurture your gifts. Take stock of how you spend your time now—your coursework, extracurriculars, or jobs. Do these things play into your gifts? Talk to people who do the jobs you're considering and see how they spend their days. Make sure the skills required actually align with your gifts. The admissions process is such a valuable opportunity to evaluate what comes easily to you and communicate to schools how you will nurture that on their campuses. At college, you can feed your gifts through the activities and jobs you choose and watch them grow and grow.

Values: They Steer Your Gifts to the Right Schools, Activities, Courses, Relationships, and Jobs

We could just leave the discussion here with doing what you love to do, but bliss is bigger than that. Remember, you're here to make a unique imprint on everyone around you. For sustained inspiration, you need to *care* about what you do *personally*, *academically*, and *professionally*. You need to bring your heart into the picture. You need to get into your values.

Values are the principles that shine like headlights on your path in this world. They aren't the morals dictated by the Greek chorus, and they aren't your mind chatter of who you think you "should" be. Instead, values come from a place deep within you, again from your *knowing* mind, not your *thinking* mind. They are what you care about and cannot live without. For example, if you discover that you have a gift for writing, it is your value of discovery that steers you towards being a reporter for the school paper or your value of helping that inspires you to become an after-school tutor. When you recognize that you have gifts for math and problem solving, it is your value of creating that steers you towards being an engineering major or your value of healing that steers you towards pre-med. It's important to see that there's no "better" path between reporter or writing tutor, between engineering or pre-med. But there is a *right* path for you.

As Gandhi is supposed to have said, "Happiness is when what you think, what you say, and what you do are in harmony." I'm not one to mess with Gandhi, but he could have tossed "feel" in there, too. There is an integrity and peace deep inside when your words and actions align with your thoughts and feelings. Along those lines as you move into your adult life, it's good to consider walking your talk, being who you say you are, doing what you truly love. As Eknath Easwaran says in his introduction to the *Bhagavad Gita* (Easwaran 2007, 64), a seminal yoga text, "Our lives are an eloquent expression of our belief; what we deem worth having, doing, attaining, being. What we strive for shows what we value."

Going off to college and becoming an adult is a big deal for many reasons; you're not really messing around anymore. Sure, you still are to a certain extent, and believe me, there are ridiculously good times to be had at college when you act your shoe size instead of your age. Yet you are moving onto a bigger stage, so to speak. What you *do* will show people who you *are*. There are so many options as to how we spend our time. Start to notice if you're frittering your energy away on things that don't really matter to you (more on this in chapter 7). Now's a good time to be more conscious about keeping your head in the game so that your life is an accurate reflection of what matters most to you.

I'm laying it on kind of thick here about the importance of values. Are you worried that you don't know what yours are? If so, then before we get into examples of values, let's do an exercise to uncover some of yours. Then we can look at why they are important and how they'll help you refine your search for bliss.

Values are solid, but they are quiet. They are deep in your heart and gut, coming from your Self. Usually, we're dragged around all day by our feelings and emotions, which are like a kick line of dancing girls sashaying across our brains. In contrast, your values are whispering in the wings of your heart, waiting for the chance to come onto center stage. You need to let yourself get still to hear them.

To explore your values, we're going to do another meditation and visualization exercise. *I know, I know, it seems so cheesy!* But once applicants start to peel away layers by considering their values, they see what's important to them, what they want to write essays about, and what they want to pursue at school. No one is going to see you do this, so don't worry about looking silly. Give it ten minutes tops. It will start off similar to the meditations we've already done. But then you're going to answer some questions. So first you'll get quiet, and then you'll open your eyes and do some writing. Seriously, ten minutes. Your heart and your essays will thank you.

How to Figure Out What's Really Important to You: A Values Awareness Exercise

Find a comfortable place to sit or lie down. (As mentioned in chapter 1, lying down holds the risk of dropping into sleepy time, but if it works for you, go for it.) If you're sitting, get some cushions or pillows to prop yourself up. Make sure you have a little time to be here to settle into the breathing. Try for at least three minutes. Also, you'll need to read through this entire exercise before you actually do it.

- Start by just breathing. Notice your inhales and your exhales. Let yourself just receive and release each breath.

- Follow your inhale up the front of your body to the top crown of your head. Follow your exhale from the top of your head back down to the base of your spine.

+ Notice that there's a slight pause at the top of the breath as you fill up, and a slight pause at the bottom as you empty everything out.

+ Take a few completely present breaths. To help your mind stay in the present moment, you can say "in" as you inhale and "out" as you exhale.

Okay, now try to close your eyes and do this for a few minutes. You can set even a timer to bring you back. Go ahead then. Set the timer. See you, bye-bye...

Now that you've opened your eyes, consider the prompt below:

Think about a time when your life was wonderful.

It could be something related to work or school, your family or an activity, or it could be social or artistic. It can be anything. Time spent alone or a time with people or with pets. Indoors or outdoors. It could be a few years or just an afternoon or just a moment. I've heard everything from being on top of a mountain to hanging with the family on summer vacation to giving a speech. It's simply a time when you felt alive and excited. Let yourself be in that time again.

After you read this, close your eyes again and spend a few moments just thinking about what you were doing and how it felt. Let yourself *be* in that moment. Imagine yourself right back there. Don't just remember it. Let yourself *feel* the energy of that experience.

Let your eyes close again. Set your timer and spend a few moments just being in that time. Bye...

Once you've spent some time being in that place, take a few moments to respond to the following questions:

+ What made that time great?

+ Why did you feel so alive?

+ What were you doing?

+ What did you enjoy?

+ What felt satisfying?

Now try that same activity with a few other questions. Choose the ones that resonate with you. Again take a few breaths, consider the question, spend time in that place, and then do a little writing.

+ What piece of schoolwork or professional work or what project are you the most proud of? What was it about you that made it possible to achieve this result?

+ What are the greatest lessons you've learned from a tough time?

+ What is a purpose you feel called to fulfill?

+ Think of a time in your life when you were angry, frustrated, or upset. What was missing?

+ Reflect back in your life to someone you have greatly admired. This can be someone you know or someone famous. What about that person—what qualities did he or she have—made you admire him or her?

Once you've thought about each of the questions, read them over. Consider your answers. What thoughts do you have as you read through them?

These types of questions can help identify your values. Consider what is important to you based on your answers. Does anything jump out? Does anything surprise you? Like the person who loved being on top of a mountain, appreciating the silence but also the challenge of the hike. Or the person who enjoyed giving the speech and saw that she loved performing and needed interactive classrooms instead of big lecture classes and long, lonely library hours. Often, when we enjoy an event or aspect of our lives, it is because it speaks to our values. Similarly, when we are dissatisfied, it is because our values are absent from a situation or relationship. It makes your life so much richer to know this about yourself so you can apply your gifts in the right direction. It also makes it much easier to show schools who you are and what's important to you when *you* know it!

Figure 2.1 is a list of sample values. As you read them, see which ones elicit a physical reaction, like an opening in your chest or a quiet confidence in your abdomen. Your body often identifies values better than your mind, so pay attention to how you physically *feel* as you read each one.

What values resonate with the satisfying times in your life? Using examples from the list in Figure 2.1 or your own words, select values that correspond with how you answered the questions. Be completely honest. This is a really important point. Let yourself be surprised by your choices. We usually have strong ideas on what we want to value. For example, one girl I know thought "leading" and "teaching" would be important to her, but all of her stories pointed to values of "beauty" and "creating." So she started focusing her efforts on activities that let her create, writing and playing piano, which would awaken her inner artist that was longing to come out. Again, your values come from a deeper place than your brain; they are bubbling up from your *knowing* mind, not your *thinking* mind.

Free yourself up to see yourself differently. All too often, we decide who we are from our heads and then just get stuck in patterns. Instead, let yourself be surprised by that list of values. What sings to you? What words get you fired up? Often you have to let go of the image you have of yourself to reveal the more genuine you. Deep down, your Self is pulling you to what will really send your heart flying. Let yourself go there.

Use these values to focus your gifts. As you get older, those gifts for singing or math may take you in many different directions. Your values will make the difference between doing what you're good at or even what you enjoy and doing what *inspires* you. When you are inspired, in your extracurriculars, courses, and jobs, then even as you face the inevitable challenges in these areas, you will want to work through them and move forward. You will feel a confidence and peace in knowing you are on the right path for you. Also, you can apply your values outside of organized school or professional settings; simply making time to feed those values in your free time and personal life will help your heart feel full.

FIGURE 2.1

VALUES*

Which of the following values are most important to *you?*

- Adventure, risk, experimentation
- Authenticity
- Beauty, grace, elegance, taste
- Impact, spark, energy
- Encouraging, ministering
- Contributing, facilitating, influencing
- Creating, design, imagination, ingenuity
- Discovering, discerning, uncovering
- Feeling, emoting, experiencing flow, sensing
- Leading, guiding, inspiring, governing
- Mastery, expertise, superiority
- Pleasure, fun, sensuality, hedonism
- Humor, laughter, play
- Relating, connecting, bonding, integrating
- Sensitivity, tenderness, compassion, empathy
- Spirituality, devotion, awakeness
- Teaching, informing, enlightening, educating, explaining
- Winning, prevailing, triumphing, accomplishing

*SOURCE: Mary Kuentz, CPCC, PCC, Coaching That Works,
  www.coachingthatworks.com.

For example, let's say your values are mastery, humor, and taste. Now you probably won't combine mastery, humor, and taste in one activity or job (although the market for funny, expert chefs does seem to be exploding with all the cooking shows). Instead, though, let's see how these values could help you apply your gifts, whatever they may be.

To respect your value of mastery, you could focus on one sport instead of playing different ones every season; you could choose a single subject major instead of an interdisciplinary one; or eventually, as a professional, you could work in a specialty role instead of a multifunctional one.

Maybe your value for humor comes out in subtle ways, like needing a smaller, more chill classroom setting or, later, a non-stuffy work environment where you're free to have witty chitchat. Or maybe you make time for humor in organized ways, like by joining an improv group. I had a friend from business school who started a company doing improv sessions in corporations to help people get more comfortable with speaking in public. Brilliant!

And as far as taste is concerned, maybe you want to be a chef or restaurant reviewer. Or maybe you just like to take time to cook a great meal and so need to find a school where you can move out of the dorms to have your own kitchen. Or maybe you need to go to school in a city where you could organize group outings to hit new restaurants, formally as a club or informally with friends.

Often, when you can't figure out why you don't enjoy something that you thought would be a good match for your gifts, it's a value that's missing. Remember the student who was a great high jumper but who really just wanted to develop her interest in dance? She clearly has values in beauty and art and performance that were missing from the jumping. Like her, just because you have a gift for teaching or math or music doesn't mean you'll tap into your bliss by doing that in just any environment.

I see this type of thing all the time with my MBA clients who have had a few different jobs. One guy felt silly because no job inspired him the way leading his college swim team did. He thought that was just a case of trying to relive his Glory Days, until he considered that the leadership was the real attraction. So he moved to a small firm where he was able to lead, and even though he was doing the same functional work as in his previous job, he was totally inspired. Another woman I worked with was a natural marketer and communicator, but she felt bored and wasn't performing well at her consulting firm, even though it was a creative and cool place. She finally answered the long-heard call of her values, which were in adventure and philanthropy; she took a huge risk and moved to South America to start a very successful women's cooperative. Now she's *way* content.

My point is that you can get a big head start on the bliss path if you can put your values into play now as you leave high school. Take a look at which values jumped out at you. You can even rank your top five. It can be hard to choose among them, I know, but usually two or three really grab you. Walk around with them in your head and heart for a bit. See if you can start to recognize areas of your life that feed these values and areas that don't—from courses to extracurriculars to jobs to relationships.

Maybe you can start putting your values into action. Look for Aha! moments on why you're drawn to different things or people based on values.

In terms of specific application advice, beyond helping you determine which extracurriculars, academic paths, and jobs (now and later) to pursue, values can help you in choosing schools. Your values come from that same knowing body of your instincts. So when you tap into your gut and heart to consider schools, let your values float around. They can help you understand why some schools feel like a good fit and others don't. A school could have the right academic, geographic, athletic, social, and artistic offerings. But if you have a value for relating to people one-on-one and the classes are huge, it may not feel good. Or if you value ingenuity but a school won't let you design your own major, then you may feel stifled.

Again, as we discussed with gifts, when you're refining your extracurricular activities around your values, remember that not everything you list or discuss in your essays or on your application needs to be an organized activity. Let's go back to that value of "taste" from before. I'm going to guess that your high school doesn't have a varsity dinner team, but you can still put "cooking" down as an activity or write an essay about it if you are doing it all the time. Tell them what types of recipes you like to try; maybe you're busy exploring different ethnic and regional cuisines. You can discuss lessons learned from experiences in this area in your essays. (We'll go into more about that in the next chapter.) For now, though, keep being true to your values as you go deeper into extracurricular activities. As with gifts, don't shy away because you can't earn a captain title or take home a trophy for being true to your values.

Now that we've done a little values work, don't just stick these thoughts in a journal and tuck them away. Values are subtler than our gifts and a bit more mysterious; they like to duck out of the way to make your life easier in terms of conforming with expectations you have for yourself (or others have for you). Sometimes, it can be hard to apply values if doing so would make your life different from how you'd imagine it should be. Keep feeding those values with some attention, however, and they will nurture you right back. Be alert to how you feel in situations, relationships, activities, and jobs and see if a value is being awakened or diminished. Acting in accordance with your values across your life is going to help you be your truest Self and let your inner light shine out.

Find Your True Callings: Put Them into Play Now, at College, and Always

Now hold onto your seat because we're about to knock this bliss thing out of the park. We've talked about how your bliss is your unique offering to the world. Again, it's not one big thing or your job or something you can put on a resume. Following your bliss is about making use of your natural gifts and applying your values across every area of your life as much as you possibly can. It's knowing who you are in your heart and being that person, instead of some version of you that you think you're supposed to be.

However, to reach chart-topping levels of bliss and truly be the biggest version of you, you need to do something for *someone else* with your gifts and values. Think about it. Consider a time when you helped someone out and consider a time when you screwed someone over. How did you feel after each one? Look, we all feel better when we do something for someone else. In fact, frequent advice given to people suffering from depression is to volunteer. In 12-step programs, participants sponsor each other down the path to wellness. Giving always brings a bigger payoff than receiving. This goes for organized service and just your general approach to the world. If you want love, give love. If you want kindness, show kindness. If you want patience, be patient. When you give out the good stuff, it comes back at you tenfold.

That doesn't mean that suddenly people are going to give you love and patience. They may, or you might have to wait a bit for the karmic circle to come back your way. But if you give love, show kindness, and have patience, you are going to feel loving and kind and patient. Immediately. That's instant karma, baby, and it will get you every time!

Again, this doesn't mean that your job has to be service or even that you should be part of some organized service. It just means listening to your heart, which is trying to tell you all the time how and when to help people. Seriously, your heart is big and ready and trying to let your Self, that divine part of you, shine out. We are each other's guardian angels. Giddyup and get helping!

We get callings all the time on how to help others. Sometimes they are quite literal. Like the other night when I came across an elderly woman struggling to make her way over a snow bank near my apartment in the West Village of New York City. She was calling out, "Can someone help me?" She might as well have had a neon sign hanging over her reading, "Get Your Instant Karma! Feel Good Now!" I helped her up, we showered each other with well wishes, and New York felt cozy and beautiful despite some man peeing on a wall about two feet from us.

Sometimes these callings are just that feeling that something is the right thing to do. One of my business school applicants called me one night totally giddy. We were going to talk about his essays, but he immediately launched into a story about one of the custodians in his office. As my applicant was often working late, he had become friends with the custodial staff doing the night cleaning. In particular, he became buddies with one man, and they shared bits and pieces of their lives. It turns out that the custodian was having some issue with his health care, but he couldn't get management to pay attention to it. The applicant intervened on his behalf and somehow got the situation resolved. He was completely thrilled that he'd been able to help. Actually, as it turns out, the applicant's manager found out about the situation and wrote something about it in his recommendation for business schools. So there was some extended karma there, but the manager could have told a million stories like this because the applicant was such a great guy. The point is that, recommendation story and extended karma or not, it's that instant thrill that you get from helping something that is the real gem in these situations. Helping people makes *you* feel better; we learned it in kindergarten, and it's totally right on. Helping others feeds your soul.

We also get bigger callings, from deep down inside. Your soul, your inner light, is always down to help the old lady in the snow so to speak; that's like batting practice for your Self. But you have much bigger things on your angel plate. Frederick Buechner (1973, 95), minister and author, said, "The place God calls you to is the place where your deep gladness and the world's deep hunger meet." Stop and think about that. Remember the Venn diagram from third-grade math? Who doesn't? It's fabulous and incredibly useful. (The intersection of Columbia and Bard is Brown!?) There is a sweet spot in the center of a Venn diagram where something that brings you joy meets up with something that people need desperately.

I'm going to play around with that a little bit here. That thing, that sweet spot, that intersection where your gladness meets the world's need, whatever it is — finding it and doing that work is going to heal you. *Say what?* I know, *heal* is a cheesy word, but stick with me here. I've been part of a lot of different service ventures in my day, and I've seen a lot of people do stuff out of a sense of obligation or duty (myself included). You know what happens: you burn out. The motivation of "doing the right thing" is not enough to sustain you over the long haul.

Instead, you need to look to that place that tugs a chord somewhere deep in you. We've all got chords inside us waiting to be tugged because they are connected to some hurt we experienced somewhere down the line. It could be an obvious connection, as for the applicant who mentored younger kids because his own dad was in jail and not around to help him. It could be subtler, as for the applicant who volunteered in political campaigns because she never felt heard as a kid. We all go through tough stuff, even if our lives look pretty easy on paper. It's just the nature of the human experience. Life is suffering, as the Buddha says, and who wants to argue with the Buddha.

Those places of pain or discontent are very powerful. In fact, that pain can either take you down, or it can inspire you to do great things. Take a look at those times of pain—but try to resist victim mode. You know how that goes: I never get to start on the soccer team because my coach is a jerk; I got dumped by that girl because she's shallow. It can feel good at first to be righteous and angry about pain others brought us or from general life circumstances, but if you get stuck in anger, you don't do yourself any favors. Anger puts you at the mercy of others or life, and it takes away your power.

If you've gone through a lot of tough stuff, your soul is giving you a crash course so you can apply lessons to help the world, pronto. Those times of darkness are necessary so you can emerge into the light. Remember, trees only grow in the valley, as my mama always said. The low points of your life bring you great teachings so you can move forward on the path to bliss. I heard playwright Eve Ensler say once: "When we give in the world what we want the most, we heal the broken part inside each of us."

Your callings—the way you serve others—are going to fix

that broken place inside of you, as well. As I've mentioned, a lot of applicants do activities to look good for college. Try to find the opportunities that actually call to you; they will help you follow your bliss. You'll also be able to explain to schools a bit about yourself by what you've chosen and the lessons you learned as you went.

Look, it's no accident this book is called *You're Accepted*. This is the book I needed to read when I was in your shoes, plus you can tell from some of my stories that self-acceptance has been a big lesson in my life. And I do a lot of things in the world around this lesson. Certainly the yoga teaching is inspired by this, as I help people feel comfortable in their own skins. Also, in day-to-day living, I love cheerleading my friends and family to follow their hearts, take risks, and be themselves. Your callings don't always translate into neat extracurricular or vocational packages, and you can tell schools about all of the things you do. Again, we'll discuss that further in the next chapter on essays. (That essay chapter is a biggie!)

However, here's one neat vocational example: I worked with an MBA applicant who knew his gifts were in finance and teaching. His values of creating and ownership were very clear. He was on the path to starting his own financial consulting firm. We also talked a lot about his passion for the underdog. The origin was pretty clear. He grew up with much less money than his friends, and he worked to put himself through private high school and college. In fact, he'd always had to work when others didn't, yet he still kept up with grades, sports, and leadership. He wasn't bitter about it; he recognized how it inspired him.

During his MBA application year, he found a place to volunteer his finance skills to get more practice, because he was working in general consulting at the time. He ended up truly helping the underdog as he advised such clients as a homeless woman who was creating her own jewelry line.

Through this work, he refined his professional goals. He wanted to specialize in advising small, start-up businesses, the kind of companies that employ most of America—and that fold very easily. He would certainly keep up the volunteer work, but he was finding a way for his job to be a vocation. His *gifts* for finance and teaching aligned with his *values* for creating his own firm, and he met the world's great hunger by advising new business.

Remember, your callings don't have to be as concrete as a book or a job or anything like that. But you have them and will continue to have them throughout your life. You will hear them from deep inside: "I want to do something about that." "This is something I can help." "I am needed in this way." They are probably connected to something you're trying to work out, or maybe it's not that obvious. Either way, you are going to hear callings. Your soul is trying to help you do your work here on earth.

Start to identify how you've already heard and answered callings through community service, courses, activities, jobs, or relationships. Brainstorm ways that you could take this to the next level. Recognize that in doing this work, you are also healing yourself. You can meet the world's great hunger every day with some aspect of yourself. You can put your gifts and values into play by befriending your neighbor, helping someone cross the street, or calling your grandma. Whatever it is, finding opportunities to celebrate your Self through helping others is the blissiest of blissful existences. Under all the human stuff, you are a soul wanting to connect and help others along their way. Don't deny it. Being you, the highest high of you, is the privilege of your life.

✦ ✦ ✦

Following your bliss is ongoing work. That's the beauty of it. Think of yourself as a seed. You're already a whole expression of who you are, but you'll keep growing into a fuller, larger manifestation of your unique Self. Now, as you reevaluate your extracurricular involvement and consider academic and professional paths, you are in a wonderful position to stop and consider how you can follow your bliss. How can you be more *you* in every aspect of your life? How can you be the truest version of your Self?

The more you use your gifts, listen to your values, and following your callings, the juicier your life becomes. You'll jump into the river of life and flow and flow and flow. We'll end back with Mr. Bliss, Joseph Campbell (1990, 214): "When you follow your bliss... doors will open where you would not have thought there would be doors, and where there wouldn't be a door for anyone else." There are doors in this world just for you. Think about it—doors just for you! Let this time of transition be an opportunity to open them up and unfold the path of your bliss.

✦ ✦ ✦

Now that you're getting ready to shine out, let's look at how to tell schools all about the fabulous you through your essays!

CHAPTER 3

❖

The Dreaded Essay

Fear Doesn't Stand a Chance against Self-Discovery

Ah, the essays. Nothing strikes more fear in the heart of applicants. "What should I write about? If I write about my trip to Madagascar to save lemur monkeys, then when do I tell them about my award-winning harmonica skills? What if I have no harmonica skills? What if I have never saved a single lemur monkey?"

I have a cartoon from the *New Yorker* tacked to the bulletin board of inspiration in front of my computer. A friend gave it to me when I began writing this book. It shows two moms and kids, post–sandbox throwdown. One mom is comforting her weeping little girl. Across the sandbox sits a pouting little boy holding an incriminating shovel. His mom is saying, "Is this the story you want to tell on your college application?"

Oh ha-ha, witty *New Yorker,* like we're thinking about college essays at age five. And yet, this scene is funny because it holds much painful truth. The pressure starting from kindergarten to get into college. The pressure of choosing the "right" essay topic. The pressure of looming parental input on essays. The pressure to make a good impression with these essays.

The essays are where the rubber really meets the road in making your application process a journey of self-discovery instead of a soulless dance for the admissions man (or woman). The essays are the only part of the application where you have full control. After all, your GPA reflects your efforts but also years of life circumstances and teacher opinions at play. Your SAT score is influenced by countless random factors, including whether you can afford to take a prep class, the temperature of the test room, and how your breakfast is sitting that morning. Your recommendations, of course, are written by the people you've asked to recommend you. (We'll chat about how to help them to help you in the next chapter, but it's still their game). In contrast, the essays are *your* show. You get to speak for yourself.

This can be terrifying: "What do they want me to write about?!" Or this can be liberating: "I get to write about me!" You can take the fear path of trying to please the admissions committees more than the student before you, or you can take a leap of faith and use the essays to learn about yourself.

One of the biggie concepts in yoga is self-study. Before you roll your eyes at the cheese factor, just give it a second. This self-study thing is going to make your essays kick butt, make the writing process a good time, and make you a more self-aware person. Remember, schools are dying to know who you actually are, so the more you can communicate that in the essays, the better! What is not to love about that?

Growing up, whenever one of my brothers was acting like a fool, say shoving a fistful of hot peppers into his mouth at a Chinese restaurant to see what would happen, the other would say, "Stop and look at yourself." Okay, maybe I was on the receiving end of this instruction as well, usually when I was dancing around the living room like an idiot. It was our code for "take a moment of self-reflection, jerk face." We were accidental yogis in this way, because stepping back to observe your own thoughts and behaviors is yoga: whether you notice that your elbows bend when you do a handstand or you recognize your fear to start your college admissions essays.

T. K. V. Desikachar (1999, 12) in *The Heart of Yoga* (a most excellent book on yoga philosophy) defines this self-study thing better than I can: "When we are swimming in a river and cannot see the bank, it is difficult to notice the current. We are moving so much with the river that we may scarcely see its flow. But if we go to the bank where we have firm ground, it is much easier to see how the river is flowing."

Ah, grasshopper, well put. Self-study is stepping back and using your inner witness to look at your thought and behavior patterns. Then you can *choose* your thoughts instead of letting your daydreams drag you around. You find the space to choose *actions* instead of just *reacting*.

And the college application essays provide an unparalleled opportunity to stop and look at yourself, if you can gather up the courage to do so. (Yep, we're back to the essays. Thanks for bearing with me.) When you write your essays, you can play this process safe and emerge with neat, clean essays that round out your application profile and probably don't tell you or the admissions committee a darn thing about you. Or you can get in there and dance around on the page, unleash your creativity, learn a few surprising things about yourself, and actually show schools what you think and feel.

If you are reading this and thinking that you aren't creative or you can't write, then I have two things to say to you: *guess again.* Creativity is pulsing through you right now waiting to come out. Even if your mind is barking that you're not creative, deep down in there, you know you are. Just letting yourself think about being creative probably feels good. It's going to feel even better unleashing it.

Writing will take some practice, and I don't mean learning how to structure a paragraph or punctuate. You've got that already. But it may take some practice to write with freedom and toss your Self out onto the page. But believe it or not, you can enjoy the practice.

Getting to know yourself through writing is, in my opinion, the best part of the application process. All of the power players in your world right now—parents, teachers, guidance counselors, and your inner achievement beast—are giving you full permission to focus on these essays. So you can take the time to do it.

If you dig deep, you can use the essay questions to look at who you are and how you became this person. You can articulate what you have learned and who you want to become. Let yourself be moved, affected, and changed by this essay-writing experience. You have complete authority to take this opportunity for significant self-study. You can shift from darkness to light in terms of understanding yourself. It's simply a matter of stepping up and taking a good look.

The Four Demons That Get in Your Way of Expressing Yourself

Ah, but were it so easy to step up and look at ourselves! As humans, we are super good at keeping ourselves in the dark. In fact, we have a few nasty accomplices that block our vision across all areas of our lives—namely, ego, attachment, aversion, and fear:

+ *Ego* is the idea that you are separate from other beings... and thus must do what it takes to protect yourself and be better.

+ *Attachment* is looking for peace or satisfaction outside of yourself.

+ *Aversion* is the flip side of attachment; you sidestep stuff you don't want to look at or deal with to stay surface-level happy-happy.

- And finally, everyone's favorite: *fear*. Oh, fear, how you scream inside our little human brains telling us we can't do this or we shouldn't do that, making us scared to reveal our beautiful, complex selves.

We've touched on these a little bit already, and we'll continue to look at them throughout the book. This chapter explores how these bad boys come into play with the writing process and looks at tips on overcoming them. Because how you do anything is how you do everything, how you approach essay writing is a good indication of how you approach your life. You can look at where ego, attachment, aversion, and fear come up in your writing process and then explore through your responses where they trip you up in life in general.

In this chapter, we'll look at these demons and ways to overcome them, and at the end, we'll look at practical ways to approach typical essay questions. So we have a little *g* goal and a big G Goal with this chapter. The (little) goal is to have some fun producing thoughtful, reflective, genuine essays; the (big) Goal is to emerge from this writing process more conscious of how you operate in the world. Ultimately, by being aware of how you hide in your "humanness," you can start to break free of that hiding to reveal more of your true Self.

In the spirit of being real and transparent, I want to say one quick thing before we dive into this work on essays. I have heard from many applicants that reading about other people's essay topics stresses them out, and I remember that feeling. It's easy to think that you'll never have topics as interesting as the examples or if you haven't lived through some great tragedy, then you have nothing to write about. So I'm going to give you some examples as we go through to help trigger your creative juices, but I'm also holding back because I don't want you to compare your life and essay ideas to others. As I'll hammer home throughout this chapter, this essay-writing process is about looking at yourself; the depth of your reflection on topics is way more important than the topics themselves. Okay, let's hit it.

Demon #1, Your Ego: Ignore It and Keep Your Writing *Real*

Appropriately enough, I've tried to start this paragraph eight zillion times and can never find the perfect, witty, illuminating example of the ego. Why? Because my own ego is preventing me from moving on until I get this just right! So in an attempt to model good ego taming, I'm just moving on here.

Look, the ego is going to try and mess with you in two main ways: demanding that your essay topics be the perfect choices and telling you that your writing needs to be perfect. If you couldn't guess already, your ego is *way* into perfection. *Way.*

But trying to be perfect is the kiss of death in your writing and in pretty much everything else in life. *No one* is perfect. What does *perfect* even mean? Who even cares? There are no perfect college essays. Even with some poorly crafted sentences and a few typos, you can still get into a fantastic school. I've seen it happen many times with UPenn, UCLA, UNC, you name it.

And you'll probably cringe when you read your essays and thoughts years from now (or later this year!), so just get over that right now.

Because by trying to be perfect, you are shooting yourself in the foot as an essay writer and as a soulful being. Your sparkling, radiant, creative Self does not get to shine when your mind is stewing over how to make your essay on feeding orphans in Peru show that you are the intelligent, sensitive, goal-oriented, and charity-minded person that you are. You are not going to learn a darn thing about yourself if you're using your essays like an advertising campaign. Moreover, those marketed essays fall flat with readers because they look, well, *marketed*.

TELL THE TRUTH

You know what's really interesting: what you actually think! What matters most to you? What do you want to do in your life? What's your favorite book? Why do you want to go to University of Georgia? Really... why?

Admissions committee members are just human beings with file folders full of essays. They want desperately to read about *you*, not some carefully manufactured version of you. They want to connect with *you*. They really want to know whom, living or dead, *you* want to have dinner with. (Personally, for the record, my choice always has been and always will be Bruce Springsteen.)

Believe me though, I understand your thinking: "But I'm trying to put forth the right image here!" You want to appear smart, polished, and worthy of your dream school. I get that. This idea haunted me big-time the first time I applied to college, and I shot myself in the foot with safe but lame essays. Though I got real with my essays when I applied to transfer, which I'll discuss in a bit, I still got tripped up in feeling that I was inadequate to represent Harvard in the real world. Because I transferred there, I've always felt like a bit of a phony. Anyway, one thing that helped me realize that I could keep it real and be worthy of Harvard was the experience of watching this dinner essay question play out in real time.

At the end of my junior year of college, I was part of a young women's leadership retreat at Rutgers University. At a lunch event with a lot of professional women mentor types, we were asked to introduce ourselves by saying whom we'd like to have dinner with, living or dead. "C'mon," I thought, "enough with the college application questions!" This super smart and super cool girl from University of Kansas went before me and said she'd want to have dinner with Hannah Arendt. *Who?* I know now, because I asked her later, that Hannah Arendt is a German political theorist. But as soon as she said it, I thought, "Oh crap, I can't say I want to have dinner with The Boss; I'm here representing Harvard, for God's sake. I have to look smart." My ego was on its knees begging me to think of something else, but I couldn't.

So I said I wanted to have dinner with Bruce Springsteen and got a lot of laughs. *Whew.* Later, though, I had not only funny but also interesting chats with the mentor types and other students about my extended family in New Jersey and Springsteen's celebration of the working person. No one seemed to think I was an idiot; in fact, just the opposite: they *complimented* me on my "refreshing take" on the question. If I had gone the poser road and said some obscure intellectual figure, I would have spent the rest of the event talking to a plant because I would have had nothing to say about my response. Telling the truth lets people in and creates connections, as I saw in real time that day. And the same rules apply for the essays.

So the big lesson here: tell the truth in your responses. Treat these essays as the incredible gifts they are and do some self-discovery. When on earth outside of third-grade journal assignments, school applications, and the occasional leadership conference do you actually think about whom, living or dead, you'd want to have dinner with? I've seen responses on this range from an applicant's deceased mom to poets to great chefs—what made each essay great was that the applicants had *real* reasons for wanting to talk to these people.

We laugh about these questions because they have become clichéd, but you really can learn a lot about yourself if you answer them for real. It can take some practice, getting real about this stuff. Maybe find a crew of friends you trust and start talking about it; drop the sarcasm and learn something about each other. While I was mentoring a group of high school seniors through a nonprofit, we did a lot of chitchatting about possible college essay topics. One night, the students and the mentors all sat around and answered supplemental essay questions for Yale, University of Virginia, and New York University: What's your favorite word? What karaoke song would you sing? What don't you like about yourself? What gives you energy? It felt like a party game because it was casual and we were all participating. As such, our responses were hilarious, serious, and totally honest.

We even called each other out when we weren't being honest. I was surprised by some of my own answers (*"Faith* is my favorite word?") and by some of theirs ("Reading about utilitarian societies really gets me going!"). We learned a ton about each other and ourselves and left wanting to know each other more and more. Getting real helps you know yourself and draws people to you. It's good for your heart and soul—and for your essays.

On that note, when you are completely honest, your essays will be incredibly personal. It may be a little scary, confusing, or strange to think honestly about these topics. Like admitting that you have a huge issue with authority and that's why your grades from freshman year aren't so hot. Or confessing to a massive need to control everything, which might be why you dig reading about utilitarian societies. Again, it's normal to meet with some resistance from your own mind. That's just your ego trying to look polished and perfect. Yawn. But if your essays make you look polished and perfect, you aren't telling the truth. You and your reader will be left bored and dissatisfied.

Often, the most compelling essays I've written or seen are so honest and revealing that the author (including me) would not share them with close friends or family (and we'll talk more about why that's a good move in a bit). Some were about dramatic stuff, like childhood abuse; others were less dramatic but still very painful, like about being discriminated against for being overweight;

others weren't painful but joyful like love for a grandparent. It's interesting that we're comfortable showing our deepest thoughts to a nameless, faceless admissions committee but not our loved ones. Again, that's our ego trying to protect us from being vulnerable. Go ahead and use the admissions committee as an anonymous slate for your expression and self-study. You don't need to worry about them being offended about how you interpreted your parents' divorce. You don't need to worry about their judgment around your secret ambitions. You can put your thoughts, hopes, and dreams into fifth gear and let 'em rip.

CHECK YOURSELF: ARE YOU REALLY KEEPING IT REAL?

So how do you go about figuring out the honest answer? I have one little test called "wake up in the middle of the night." Basically, the honest answer is the one you would say if someone woke you up in the middle of the night and asked the question. It's the answer from your heart.

Here's an example from a client I had who was applying to Stanford's Graduate School of Business. For years, Stanford's first application question has been "What matters most to you and why?" It's notorious. People fear it. It's fabulous! What an awesome thing to sit around and think about. In this life you've got going on, what matters the most to you? It's a massive, soulful question. This particular client wanted to say, "Integrity." Really? I asked him if someone woke him up in the middle of the night and screamed, "What matters most to you?" would he shout out, "Integrity"?

Of course, he reconsidered, and he confessed that he liked "integrity" because it would let him talk about all of these different aspects of his life where he'd been successful. He was on his way to writing an editorialized version of his resume. No lessons learned for him; no revealing of his values to the admissions committee.

After some thought, he decided it was his grandpa that really mattered most to him. It made him emotional just to think about their relationship. Feeling emotions like vulnerability or being afraid that you're getting too personal are all great signs that you're on the right track. He still wanted to talk about integrity because he learned that from his grandpa, but now he was telling the truth. He had found a genuine human side to his answer. That emotional deep dig helped him learn something about himself and how he'd become the young man he was. In coming from an honest, personal angle, he came across as vulnerable, insightful, and real to anyone reading his essay.

When you start telling the truth in your responses, you will probably surprise yourself with your topics. The answers to these essay questions can be simple, complex, or even something that you don't think you should talk about. Whether you're writing about your dog, running on the boardwalk, or overcoming stuttering, just allow yourself to speak your heartfelt truth.

One other point on keeping it real: tell the truth in your essays in terms of the facts you state. *Don't claim to be anything that you aren't.* And *don't say you've done something that you haven't.* Not lying in essays should a no-brainer. But I've seen some otherwise very well-intentioned, ethical people get tempted by their competitive egos to stretch the truth or exaggerate. Please don't. Save those skills for the short story or novel you might want to write. Seriously. If you weren't the leader of a team, then don't play it off like you were. If you didn't come up with the great idea that turned around the class project, then don't say you did. That stuff is lying. It will make you feel gross for doing it (karma at play), and it won't help your application. As we'll discuss in a bit, your reflections on events and experiences are the real key to essays, so you aren't even helping your application by ramping up the facts. Enough said.

KEEP IN MIND THAT EVERY STORY HAS TWO SIDES

Finally, in keeping it real, open yourself up to the fact that you can be wrong. Ouch. Some of these essays ask you to explore a current event or one of your beliefs. And oh the ego loves to be right, right, right on this kind of thing. Yet for every belief and opinion you carry around in your busy human brain, someone else disagrees wholeheartedly and can debate you into the ground. Part of telling the truth is accepting that there is no truth. Whoa. Got kind of meta there. But true: there are divergent opinions on everything. See if you can take a stand but acknowledge the other side. This also comes up when you describe personal experiences, as with an applicant who wanted to criticize her peers on a volunteer project to show how she stepped up and took the lead. Keep to your story; you have no idea what other people were thinking and feeling and what their motivations were. Remember, the essays are about you.

The essays are a great training ground for college classes in this way. Most of the time in college, you're practicing critical thought—being able to explore an issue from a variety of angles, hearing what other people have to say, and coming to understand their perspectives. Your essays are a great opportunity to see your own discomfort or willingness to be flexible in this way. So practice arguing your points and then give it a go from the other side. See your point of view but don't assume what others are thinking. It's great training for releasing the ego's grasp on the rightness of your human thoughts and behaviors.

On that note, keep an open mind regarding any and all essay advice that you hear. But, *my* truth is to tell you to express *your* truth. From top to bottom, keep your ego in check and keep your essays real. Tell the truth in big and small ways. It is such a waste of your natural creativity to get tripped up in trying to be anything other than you in all of your glowing and growing glory. Answer the questions for you, not for the admissions committee. See what you can learn about yourself in doing so. By keeping it real, you are taking a first step towards fun and fascinating essays and a big step ahead in life.

Demon #2, Attachment:
Find Out *Why* You Chose This Topic

Now that I've done a whole song and dance about honesty in choosing your topics, I have to be honest: the topic you choose isn't really that important. All of the questions are essentially just asking you who you are. Thus, the real kicker is *why* you choose the topic. You can write a boring and shallow essay about building houses in Africa or a revealing and insightful essay about sitting on the bench of your high school basketball team. I've seen both. I've found the difference between surface essays and those that do a deeper dive is writers' willingness to be surprised by their own stories.

Tragically, we often decide who we are and how our lives will go based on old stories we tell ourselves about ourselves. In clinging to these patterns, we end up playing things very small. This essay-writing process is great practice for releasing your current impressions of yourself. Let yourself get very curious about your true nature, your bigness, your heart, all that resides within you. To do so, let your Self take you by surprise. Don't be so quick to write the same old stories about you.

KEEP ASKING YOURSELF WHY? WHY? WHY? UNTIL YOU FIND THE HEART OF YOUR TOPIC

The key to learning about yourself and, thus, putting out an interesting essay, is to look at the why and how behind all of your responses. For example, I had one applicant through my nonprofit work who had a nice, well-written essay about her messy room. However, it was a gimmicky essay: she was just listing all of the stuff in her room to show all of her diverse interests to the admissions committee. She had her "story" that she was messy—that was her idea of taking a risk and not being perfect—and from there she could list all of her activities (which a school would see in her forms anyway).

So instead of sticking with that, we got into a discussion about *why* her room was a mess. We really pushed it. Of course, there was the passive-aggressive battle with her mom over the messiness, a battle she didn't want to lose. We kept going though, getting curious about why she had so many things from childhood stored in her room.

After mulling it over for a while, she recognized a Peter Pan syndrome: she was hesitant to grow up. Of course, this had been playing out across her life in other ways: she was hesitant to make her final list of schools, she was hesitant to start writing essays. The reality of leaving high school, going to college… it all felt like a lot to her, and she was scared.

What followed was an awesome revision of that essay that got much deeper into her hesitations about growing up and moving forward. It revealed a connection to her hometown, which she claimed to hate. It was really beautiful and totally surprising to her. It wasn't the way she usually looked at herself, and her heart came bursting out. There was some sadness and great humor. She had to be willing to push the boundaries a bit and get vulnerable in exploring her topic. She had to let go of that girl with the neat extracurricular evidence scattered around her room and reveal the girl with the big, complicated, open, honest heart, Peter Pan syndrome and all.

I had another applicant, this time for business schools, whose biggest challenge was speaking in public: from third-grade book reports to high school and college club leadership to work presentations. Despite this truth, she resisted discussing this in her business school applications—for a good reason, because all you do in business school is speak in public every day! Since that's the primary teaching method, why would she tell the admissions committee that she struggles with the very thing she is applying to do all day long?

The first reason she needed to write about this is because it was the wake-up-in-the-middle-of-the-night answer and, thus, the honest response. Moreover, when she dug deeper into how this issue developed, it opened up self-reflection about insecurity and a need for control that stemmed from some interesting family challenges she'd had as a kid. In fact, although these issues presented themselves most fully around public speaking, the insecurity and need for control spilled over into her whole life and influenced her decisions. By writing the essay and putting everything out in the open, she connected dots about how these issues may have hurt her in the past but how she wanted to use the lessons learned to move forward in the future. Ultimately, she wrote a really hopeful and fascinating essay about way more than speaking in public, and now she's graduated from Harvard Business School, the grand-daddy of public speaking environments.

You know how little kids will just go and go with the *why, why, why, how, how, how?* In his early years, my nephew pushed my brother to his existential limits in trying to answer all the *why's* and *how's*. You need to channel *your* inner two-year-old. Each of your experiences is about much more than that experience. It's back to how you do anything is how you do everything. Your fears are wrapped up in your messy room. Your values are coming out in your issues with public speaking. If you really probe yourself to find the why, you will learn about how you live your life, not just what three books you'd bring if you were on a desert island. Allow yourself to be surprised by the connections you make. Take a step back and see yourself in a new and deeper way.

YOUR ESSAY SHOULD BE ALL ABOUT YOU:
DON'T LET ANYONE ELSE INFLUENCE WHAT YOU WRITE

Perhaps even harder than releasing from your attachment to how you see yourself is letting go of how people close to you see you. This may seem like an obvious point, but *you* decide the topics and responses for your essay questions, not other people.

For example, another of my applicants through my nonprofit work has incredible experience but is a little weak in grades and scores. I was helping him think through how to address this; we'd even outlined many of his essays. Then he wasn't delivering on writing anything. There was a lot of stuff going on for him at home, but still, deadlines were looming.

After I kept bugging him, he sent me a letter he had written to a teacher a few months ago that could work as an essay. It was nothing like what we had outlined, but it was one of the most creative and bravest essays I'd seen in my years of doing this. His language was free and poetic, and he was willing to show unattractive habits and feelings and complex lessons learned. He knew what he wanted to write. He didn't want to follow those outlines. It just took a while for him to get brave enough to show it to me, the so-called expert on this stuff.

I was so proud of him for mustering up his courage and disregarding our work. He put his heart before my opinion and discovered much more about himself, and created a killer essay, in
the process. Bravo!

FORGET ABOUT YOUR AUDIENCE: THIS IS *WRITING*, NOT EDITING

Once you've chosen your topic, you can fall into the trap of self-
editing while you write. You wonder what the people in your life
would think of your writing, and you try to keep them happy
as you go. I know you do this, because everyone does (myself
included!). But your college essays are great practice for letting go
of that self-editing button in general. They are a chance for you
to express your revelations, hopes, and dreams without worrying
about approval from your close family and friends. Putting those
thoughts down in their full glory is a first step towards letting go
of what others think and instead living straight from your heart
and Self.

Again, you are going to send all of this work to an anonymous
audience. Try to take advantage of that. I mentioned earlier in this
chapter that many applicants write such personal things that they
don't want anyone in their lives to read them. This is actually a
good sign that you're getting into some fresh ideas about who you
are. Your essays should be as personal as your diary or journal in
terms of your honesty and freedom in your self-expression. Do
you let your family read that?

Soapbox moment: I encourage you not to let parents, brothers, sisters, or close friends currently applying read your essays. It's too hard for them to read your work without their own filters. It's probably impossible. In my experience every time — *every time* — an applicant gives an essay to a parent or even a sibling, it comes back with all of the juicy, interesting stuff edited out. Either the applicant was scared to show the real stuff, or the reader challenged the applicant on it. It's a bummer. I completely shot myself in the foot with this the first time I applied to colleges (details on my two different essay approaches coming in a bit). It can be great to get another set of eyes on what you've written, but try to find an impartial source, whether it's an adult at school or a mentor through another venue. If possible, try to find readers who are a few steps removed from your life, like teachers, a coach, a boss, or older friends who have been through the process. (We'll talk about some of these helpful folks in chapter 4.)

Finally, this is a great chance to let go of your impressions of yourself as a writer. Perhaps you've had a very free and flowing experience with writing thus far in your life. If so, awesome. If not, though, now can be a time to fancy yourself a writer and really enter that head space. We'll get into this a bit more at the end of this chapter with some writing exercises. Just plant the seed now that you can let go and get raw, wild, bold, messy, and risky as you work yourself into these essays. It will be delicious.

Demon #3, Aversion: Don't Overprotect Yourself; Take a Risk!.

Aversion is *attachment*'s partner in crime against revealing your true Self. Because we attach to our ego, we want to do whatever it takes to keep it intact. We forget that our hearts that are bigger and bolder than our busy brains and perfectionist egos. To self-protect, we avoid things that have or may hurt us. This self-protection can be really important and helpful.

Most people have some traumatic stuff happen to them, especially when we're kids. I'm defining *trauma* really broadly here. A situation that could be no big deal to a friend could be life altering for you. Doesn't mean anything other than it's all relative. We all need a certain level of self-protection to just make it through life.

SHINE SOME LIGHT ON THE DARK AREAS OF YOUR LIFE

Unfortunately, our attachment to protecting ourselves and avoiding risks becomes a pattern. We develop fear and shame voices in our heads. We deem parts of ourselves unacceptable, and we try not to show them in public or deal with them in private. However, if you continually avoid this stuff, it can really drag you down. In this sense, you are still attached to what you are avoiding. As stated earlier, what you resist, persists. You cannot get past these blocks unless you confront them. In the meantime, these limiting voices in your head prevent you from fully expressing your emotions, developing your gifts, or pursuing your dreams. This comfortable aversion comes at a big cost to your Self.

It also affects your essays to the extent that you try not to look at certain parts of yourself or your life — for example, not wanting to confess that you have an issue with authority and, thus, are not perfect, avoiding writing about a difficult period in your life or family, or just limiting yourself from being truly honest and free in your writing and responses. You'll be able to see when these voices of self-protection come up. Your writing will fall flat. You'll feel a lack of energy. You'll get bored writing and reading your own work, because it will sound *safe*.

The good news is that if you give the dark parts of yourself some attention, there's usually a lot of energy, wisdom, and insight there. In your essay writing, when you shine a light on this murky stuff, you may find new, deeper sides to yourself and release some blocks. When you open yourself up to learn something, these difficult people and experiences become our best teachers.

In fact, these darker parts of ourselves and times in our lives are usually connected to some deep soul purposes we have here in the school of life. Remember those callings from the last chapter. At some level, your Self is raring to shine some serious light in this world. But your human self had to go through some darkness to learn lessons to share. So these tough times that we're avoiding actually have some massive importance in our lives — and writing about them can really help you move forward on the lessons-learned front.

This does not mean you should write essays bemoaning your parents for loving your brother more than you or complaining about being the only scholarship kid at your expensive high school.

While you may write about your sibling rivalry, being a scholar-ship student, or, having a picture-perfect family and not needing a scholarship, the point is to examine how you grew from any of the big experiences or relationships in your life. It's that reflec-tion and learning that can help you grow through writing juicy, illuminating essays.

WRITE A "HERO'S JOURNEY"

To help you move from a place of victimhood to one of self-aware-ness, maturity, and inspiration, we can use a model that you'll recognize from countless books like Homer's *Odyssey* or movies like *Star Wars*. It's called "the hero's journey." Not my phrase. It's a well-known structure. (Actually, it's what the writer of *Star Wars* George Lucas borrowed from our bliss man Joseph Campbell). Here's how it goes.

The hero starts off just innocently living life. Then there's some call to action, like defeating darkness in the universe or, say, getting dumped. The hero goes through an initiation and takes on challenges, like battling Darth Vader or having to see your ex-boyfriend date some other girl at school. There are allies along the way to help the hero, be it Yoda or your best friend. Then there's a breakthrough moment when the hero emerges from darkness into light, the universe is saved, or you realize that the heartbreaker is just another dude who will one day be lonely in a library study-ing physics and you have your own fantastic life to lead. Finally, the hero has a celebration and sees the lessons learned and value of the journey.

We all go through journeys like this many times in our lives. We face heartbreak, illnesses, loss of loved ones, betrayals, abuses, divorces, defeats, and it goes on and on. Some of these experiences roll right off of us, and some of them stick with us. It's in the ones that stick where you may have some deeper lessons to explore. Karmically speaking, you have some valuable lessons to learn here.

Writing provides you with a platform to do some thinking and explore what wisdom can be gleaned from these tough times. Again, remember those callings we talked about in chapter 2? Often our callings come from these big challenges. As we discussed, in following your callings, you are probably healing some part of you. You're shining light on some dark place so that energy can instead become power behind your gifts, talents, and light in the world.

Take a moment and think about a time when you went through a hero's journey, and try to identify the different parts. Scribble a few ideas down in Figure 3.1, just to get started. (And if you don't want anyone to see what you've written in this book, scribble your ideas on any piece of paper that's nearby—and then keep it for your eyes only when you're done.)

When you start to look at your life more symbolically, you can see the lessons, and how you get to know your Self and your power a little better with each test. Through exploring these tests in writing, you can see how you're not just a victim in life. Instead, you're processing the lessons learned and getting closer to your truth. This wisdom will come across in your essays. Schools will see your maturity, self-awareness, and courage in your willingness to look at tough stuff from a framework of change and growth.

FIGURE 3.1

THE HERO'S JOURNEY

+ Innocence:

+ Call to Action:

+ Initiation:

+ Allies:

+ Breakthrough:

+ Celebration:

Throughout the years, I have seen some really powerful essays that came from these types of situations: essays about having a brother who has Down syndrome, being sexually abused by an older sibling, being the only poor kid at a fancy private high school, having a father in prison, losing a parent to cancer, dealing with parents' divorces, watching parents lose all of their money, moving a bunch of times as a kid, getting teased for being unattractive, feeling ostracized because of religious background. The list could go on and on. I give these examples not to say that you *have* to write about something painful but rather to let you know that you *can*. Remember, what made each of these essays so powerful was not the subject but the learning that came for the writer. This is a very important point: the applicant didn't focus on the situation but rather on what he or she learned and how he or she grew up because of it. In each case, the writer emerged different, healed, and inspired by life lessons. Many of the writers developed new ideas for vocations or philanthropic work based on these experiences. Your soul callings often come from the tough stuff.

AGAIN, YOUR ESSAY SHOULD BE ABOUT *YOU*

From the examples above, it's clear that childhood and families are rich with material, which is another reason why it's not the best idea to have your family or closest friends read your essays. I know I'm hammering home this point, but if you write your essays thinking about family or close friends reading them, you'll kill your spirit and your words.

As an example, I will share my tale of college essays gone

wrong, which requires a brief bit of background on my family. Give me just a minute here to explain. A couple of weeks before I entered high school, my parents got separated. If you've been through this, you know how much it hurts and how confusing it is. Simply put, it was a huge bummer. I thought the golden retriever puppy my mom bought me that summer was a replacement for my brothers who would now both be away at college, leaving me alone with my parents for the first time. Turns out my dad was leaving, too. I was super pissed—at my parents for screwing this up, at my brothers for leaving me with this mess, and at all adults for being idiots. Mind you, though, I was a classic good girl, a "perfect" child who never wanted to rock the boat. So my healthy anger, frustration, and disillusionment went unexpressed. Oh the repression! My parents actually worked things out, and my dad moved back home about halfway through my freshman year of high school. Though their reconciliation was what I desperately wanted, for a 13-year-old girl, perhaps the only thing more annoying that watching your parents separate is watching them date and get back together. That year was rough for me, and my emotions and grades reflected it. But I never talked about it.

As a sophomore, I wrote a speech about my parents' separation and reconciliation, mostly focusing on how my new dog Daisy taught me about forgiveness, grace, and compassion in the face of my parents' fallibility and vulnerability. Hey, when the student is ready, the teacher appears, even in fluffy, four-legged form. My speech teacher loved it and submitted it to a competition. I can't quite remember the details, but I think the competition involved leaving school during the day, which required a parent permission slip. I hadn't told my parents about the speech, because it was private and emotional, and as I said, I rarely expressed emotions other than happy-happy. Though I didn't go to the competition, I did show my mom the speech. I remember her being upset and saying that my perceptions of them during that time weren't accurate. She probably wasn't even that upset or upset at all. I was just such a people-pleaser that I didn't want to make anyone slightly upset ever. But I do remember thinking that my perceptions were mine—and perhaps I shouldn't share the darker ones anymore.

So when it came time to write my college essays, my supportive, generous parents were on deck to proofread and offer feedback. Thus, the topics I chose and my reflections would be totally open to them. This was tricky for me. Not that I wanted to write about their separation, or maybe I would have, but I didn't want them to know all of the inner and not so shiny, happy workings of my increasingly independent mind. I should have been brave enough to tell them I wanted to keep my thoughts personal; they were just trying to help as much as they could. Instead, I avoided any deep thoughts and wrote some lame essay about my summer swim team. Moreover, I didn't explain to colleges why my grades freshman year were much lower than my later grades. When schools see that stuff, they just want to understand what happened. But I didn't tell them. Also, because I wasn't particularly passionate about my school list, I struggled with the essays on why I wanted to go to each school and relied on basic stuff like size and maybe geography (though my list was completely inconsistent on those fronts). I was so terrified of not being perfect that the whole essay-writing process was miserable and stressful and just something to get done.

Several years later, in contrast, I treated my transfer applications to Brown, Wesleyan, Bowdoin, and especially Harvard like a big Hail Mary. Toss 'em out and see what happens. Look, the worst had gone down. I'd gone to a school I didn't like, had a total meltdown, dropped out of college, and moved home. May as well show them what I'd learned. As such, I went a buck wild with the essays, meaning I answered them honestly. I also kept them for my eyes only — and, of course, the nameless, faceless admissions committee. But I was my main audience. I indulged and took my time and wrote real, vulnerable essays about having a breakdown and letting perfectionism slip from my grasp. I discussed my newfound feminism and how I was affected by courses at Northwestern, certain books, and my work at NOW. I was specific about why each school would be a good fit for me and why I was dissatisfied with Northwestern. I knew that I could return to Northwestern after this period of reflection and it would be fine. But I didn't want fine. I wanted to thrive. I knew college would shape my adult self. I wanted to play it big at the place that was right for me.

I had two very different essay-writing experiences, and with my real, risky transfer essays I was accepted by each school. But because it takes time to learn lessons, my graduate school applications paralleled my undergraduate experience. I was tight and formal in my law school essays and didn't get into my top schools.

I was loose and real in my business school essays and got into all three schools, Harvard, Yale, and Stanford. The overall point is that I used those transfer and business school essays for self-discovery. They affected me and helped me grow up. Learn from my mistakes! Be you and be real and address the tough stuff.

Over the years, I've talked to so many people about essays for college, business and law school, and Teach For America, either in a professional capacity or just giving advice. Everyone wants to avoid writing about tough topics because they are scared or they think they can't write about them in an interesting and powerful way. But you can do it. You just need to write these essays for *you*. If you dare to write about the hard stuff and explore these darker stories, you will be changed and lighter and brighter for it.

Demon #4, Fear: To Overcome It, You Just Need to Write, Write, Write

I wonder what it's like to be afraid of writing. Oh, that would be what I feel every minute of every day right now! Don't get me wrong. I do love writing, but it also scares the wee-wee out of me. There have been whole days creating this book where I mostly just stared at my computer and wept. For real, folks: if I thought anyone was actually going to read these words other than my editor, then I would be totally paralyzed. Actually, it freaks me out that even he will read this. When I write, I use a super big font, like 200 percent, in an attempt to save my eyes. (Never mind that I'll be totally deaf in about five years from iPod abuse while walking around New York.) Anyhoo, this grandma-sized font means

I can see only a couple of paragraphs of text at a time on the screen. Often, I find myself in the predicament that I've written all the stuff but it's in the wrong order, so I have to jigsaw puzzle it around. You know how that goes right? The other day, I put my work into regular-sized font to see more of it on the page for said jigsawing. The text suddenly looked like a real live book! I got so freaked out that I went back to the big font immediately.

FEEL THE FEAR, AND WRITE YOUR ESSAY ANYWAY

Fear is huge. It's massive, ugly and lovely, and totally important in our lives. Fear (as discussed in yoga philosophy) is technically the fear of losing our lives. It's the idea that we cling to our bodily life. Note your resistance to, say, walking backwards off a cliff. A less dramatic way to think of fear is that it is clinging to the known, being afraid to let go of familiar patterns. Because when you do free yourself from these habits and patterns, in a sense, you are letting an old part of you die. You are finding a new freedom—a new life, so to speak. These endings and beginnings can be taking big risks or making small shifts. In each moment, though, you have the chance to let old stuff go and begin anew. Awesome, no?

Fear is going to stare you down as you begin this essay-writing process. It will come at you with a series of wicked karate chops. You won't be able to start writing because you are too busy, lazy, stumped, cocky, annoyed, distracted, hungry, tired, whatever (more on obstacles in general in chapter 5). Then the demons I just described will rear their ugly heads. Your *ego* will tell you things have to be perfect. You'll be *attached* to certain ideas of how your writing should go and what you'll say. You'll *avoid* getting into the messiness of real emotions. And it all comes together in a big *fear* cocktail: you'll be scared to free yourself to see what you can do, who you can be, when you are unleashed on the page.

One of my best friends, who is a fabulous writer, told me when I began this book that I should write and write and write. This has been the most important tip I've received. Because when all else fails, just take the pressure off and go. See what can happen when you just go and go and go. This is a biggie for the perfectionists out there. You can always *rewrite*. First, though, you have to *write*. None of it comes out like you think it should. Who cares? Just put it out there.

WRITING GETS BETTER IF YOU KEEP WRITING (SO PRACTICE, PRACTICE, PRACTICE!)

Before you go diving headfirst into essay topics, start by priming your writing pump. Writing may or may not feel like a natural gift. Some folks dig it, and others don't. No matter whether or not your fifth-grade teacher told you were a good writer, you can write. You may not win a Pulitzer, but you can express yourself on paper. It will help you across the board in life to start writing more.

I encourage every applicant to start writing in a journal before getting anywhere near essay topics. Yes, a journal … and if you've never kept a diary or written in a journal, and even if you think it's stupid or silly or weird, do it anyway. Nobody needs to read what you're writing, you don't need to journal about anything heavy, and you certainly shouldn't journal about the essay topics if they don't sing to you just yet. If you haven't done this before, take time to get yourself a journal that you like. It can be fancy or not fancy: even a spiral notebook will work. Just make sure you're not afraid to write in it. (I've had a few journals whose covers were so lovely that I didn't think my measly thoughts were worthy of them—that doesn't help!)

Then make time each day just to practice writing about you and your life. In her excellent book *Writing Down the Bones*, Natalie Goldberg (1986, 11) says, "Through practice you actually do get better. You learn to trust yourself more and not give in to your voice that wants to avoid writing. It is odd that we never question the feasibility of a football team practicing long hours for one game; yet in writing we rarely give ourselves the space for practice." How true is that?

Here are a few ways to get started:

- *Write down ten things you're grateful for every day.* Oprah made this "gratitude journal" idea popular, and it will make you a happier, shinier person (really). Gratitude is one of the big keys to happiness. You can write about whatever you want. Big things or small things. Events, people, or simple moments. In my gratitude journal, you'll find repeated shout-outs to the nice woman from the laundry place, my awesome superintendent, and the friendly doorman down the street who meets my smile and wave with, "All right, dear. Have a lovely day!" Though they might be surprised (or even creeped out) to know they are in my journal, most days what I am grateful for amidst the hustle of New York City is the people who make my life feel like a cozy episode of Sesame Street. Get creative in your simplicity about what makes you happy each day.

- *Write down three lessons and three blessings from your day.* Again, these can be big or small. They can even be the same things every day. As we know, it can take a lot of repetition to learn life's lessons!

- *Write down your first thoughts in the morning.* My best friend from college is a singer/songwriter who gets some of her greatest material from these drowsy, dreamy first thoughts of the morning.

- *Write down what's keeping you up at night before you get in bed.* Some of my more stressed-out applicants find that this even helps them sleep. (And as we'll discuss in chapter 5, getting enough sleep is especially critical when you're stressed out, and applying to college is, as you know, a very stressful time.) Once you write out issues, the energy goes away from them, so you can drift off without their churning around in your head.

- *Write down all the bummer experiences you've had, or write out angry letters you want to send to people who have done you wrong.* I love this one. Then throw them away or burn them! Just getting the anger out there usually diffuses it and helps you move on.

- *Write down great quotes or things you learn from books or magazines you're reading.* When I read Bill Clinton's autobiography, I was stunned by how much he remembered about what he was reading and thinking about when he was at Oxford. I'm guessing he was keeping journals. You'd better start now so we can enjoy your 900-page autobiography down the line!

READING MORE ALSO HELPS YOU WRITE BETTER

On that note, another great way to prepare for essay writing is to start reading more. Read whatever you want; just put more words into your life. Seeing thoughts and how they are composed will nudge you into writing mode. I know you're probably feeling overwhelmed by all the books you have to read for school, but also take time to read what you want. The library lends books for free! It's genius!

This may all sound like advice for a fourth grader, but I swear it helps. In my work with admissions clients, I have come across some extremely reluctant writers, a lot of math types who were terrified of essays. Many of them became some of the best writers I've seen once they started reading more and journaling. Ultimately, they fell in love with writing and came up with really creative, heart-filled essays about cooking, soccer, whatever. A piece of their spirit just woke up when they started writing in their journals and then their essays.

TRY TO HAVE FUN WITH YOUR WRITING: IT DOESN'T HAVE TO BE A CHORE

My parents' minister always says it's a good sermon if he makes them cry and he makes them laugh. I think that applies to admissions essays, too. Except I want to spin that slightly. You should make yourself cry, or laugh, or both when you're reading your *own* essays. Having that kind of emotional reaction means that you're not only tapping into truth but also enjoying the process. Part of engaging in this soul gazing and self-study is letting your personality shine through.

You'll spend most of your college and professional life creating a lot of documents that have nothing to do with you. Your soul and personality will have to sit in a desk drawer while you analyze books, compute problem sets, and fumble through PowerPoint. Doing that stuff isn't necessarily a bad time and you'll learn many things, but you probably won't be learning much about yourself.

So now is your chance. Let's face it: we are a culture that needs permission from authority to indulge in anything other than work. So celebrate the fact that admissions essays offer you full permission to ponder questions to the depths of your soul and write with the joy of your personality. You're even allowed to put school or work on the back burner while you tend to the stew of essays. Get in there, chomp it up, and have a good time.

Although the point I'm making is about enjoying the present moment and focusing on the efforts, I'll also appeal to the practical voice in your head. You also want to show your personality because the admissions committee is begging to see it. Do you know what's worse than writing a bunch of lifeless admissions essays? *Reading them*. I've been there. They are dying to see something that makes them laugh, warms their hearts, or makes them think—*anything* to see real people behind this heavily edited prose. So throw them a bone. And have some fun!

BECOME A WRITER

What makes someone a writer? I've been thinking about this a lot lately because when people ask me what I'm doing professionally these days (it's always changing!), I have a hard time saying I'm a writer. I can say I'm a yoga teacher because I show up at Yoga Works or Equinox, teach people, and get a check. Though I have a publisher for this book, I still have trouble saying I'm a writer. The degree-getting part of my brain is hesitant to say, "I'm a writer," because I haven't received formal training. So who gets to claim the title of Writer? Do you have to be paid to be a writer? Do you have to be published? Do you have to be only writing and not doing anything else? Must you write a certain number of hours each day?

Don't be me. Claim the identity of writer right now! If you write, then you're a writer. You go to high school, so you're a student. You play softball, so you're a softball player. You tutor kids, so you're a tutor. You write, so you're a writer. Simple as that. Take that title of writer seriously—without taking any of your writing seriously. If you're fortunate, you'll be able to spend a lot of time writing as you take on the college essays. The more time you spend doing it, the less pressure filled it will seem. Write in your journal, tinker around with essay topics, revise your work. Step into the feeling of becoming a writer. Play with words, get free flowing and freewheeling as you toss stuff onto a page. You will always come up with more. Your ideas are boundless.

You can be a writer your whole life. It doesn't matter how you're paying your rent. You can always be a writer. The page is a very special place, a place to explore and discover and challenge yourself. Let your career as a writer begin now. Congratulations!

Typical Essay Topics

Taking the first step with these things is often the hardest part. You're all fueled up to do some self-discovery. You're ready to shush your ego, release your perfectionism, let go of old stories about yourself, get messy with tricky times in your life, play around in your journal, and be a writer. Um, but how do I start these essays? Fair point.

Let's look at some of the common types of essay questions and how you can approach them in a way that lets *you* come out on the page.

Essay Question Type 1: Who are you?

Examples of these questions include the following:

+ Write a personal statement.
+ What's an important extracurricular?
+ What do you do in your spare time?

+ If you could meet anyone, who would it be?

+ What's an important issue to you?

+ Who has influenced you?

+ How will you bring diversity to campus?

This is the most common type of undergraduate application question, and it's the most fun. These questions give you a chance to celebrate your personality and explore your varied interests. The age-old writing advice is to *show* rather than tell, and that's big-time important with these essays. Give specific examples that illustrate who you are. In approaching these essays, take time to look across your life and think about your priorities, significant experiences, and any complicated areas in your background.

To get started, try brainstorming significant moments in your life from childhood to the present. These can come from family experiences, travel, school, work, or community service. Let go of the stories you thought you'd tell about yourself in your essays and get curious about times that stick with you. Look for patterns in your gifts and values. See if there are callings that you answered or want to answer.

If the question is broad, you may want to use a few micro examples, significant moments from your life that weave together a theme. If the question is more specific, then you may just have one example but show how it relates to the whole of your life or how it is representative of you and your personality.

These essays are true gems for self-discovery. Your gifts and values will be all over these important aspects of your life. You can do a deep dive into the experiences and relationships that have shaped and changed you. Express who you are becoming and how you hope to grow as a college student and after graduation.

Essay Question Type 2:
Give an example of you in action?

Here are some examples of these questions:

+ Describe a time when you acted as a leader.
+ Give us an example of your participation on a team.
+ What is the greatest challenge you've faced?
+ What is your greatest accomplishment?

The big pitfall in the "tell us about a time" questions is telling them about the time. All too often, these essays become long, detailed explanations of sports games or volunteer events or work projects. Recounting the specifics of your choir concert isn't going to teach you anything about yourself. Just set up the event quickly and then focus on your *experience* during that time—how you felt, what you did, and what you learned. Use these essays to consider how you react to situations and how you grow from experiences. If you get into details, let them be about your feelings. Examine your emotions during and after these big events.

Also, these questions are great opportunities to practice non-attachment to the stories you usually tell about yourself. Explore all aspects of your background (academic, family, volunteer, athletic, work), and be honest about what times have truly demanded something of you. Discover and reflect on those moments in your life that have brought out your resilience, vision, creativity, and determination. Consider how your past behavior has informed your current approach to life and how you hope to grow during your future school experience.

Think about what inspires you to lead a group of people or make a difference. What specific gifts help you make things happen? Not everyone's are the same, obviously. Some folks are more out-in-front types, while others act with greater subtlety. Neither is better. Start to know yourself.

Finally, consider what challenges and accomplishments really speak to your soul. Remember your hero's journeys. Pull out your lessons learned. Think expansively about what an accomplishment is in your life, like helping a friend, developing a relationship with your grandma, or keeping a good attitude while working a not-so-inspiring job (boring or challenging jobs can make for great essays because you tend to learn so much about yourself in these situations; just stay focused on lessons learned rather than complaining). Your topics may not deal with what you've traditionally considered accomplishments. I know you want schools to see that stuff, but they will. There are places on the application to put down awards and such. In contrast, the essays are for exploring your *feelings* around events. Consider how you've grown up because of certain events, and use this as an opportunity to explore gratitude.

Essay Question Type 3:
What do you want to do in life?

Examples of these questions are these:

- Why do you want to go to this school?

- What are your short- and long-term goals?

- Describe your job/extracurricular/academic experience: how has it influenced your goals?

These questions offer the perfect opportunity to consider how you are putting your gifts, values, and callings into play in your life. Take time to explain to yourself how your goals reflect what is important to you. This does not mean your goals and values exactly coincide necessarily, just that there is some correlation. See if the goals you bring up in this essay echo the themes that come up in your other essays. If the gifts and values you discuss in your essays about "who you are" aren't reflected in the schools you're choosing or the goals you're planning, then you can consider the discrepancies. Take this opportunity to see if you are planning a life that aligns with who you truly are.

For questions about why you want to go to a particular school, the person you should be convincing is *you*! How will your gifts grow there? How do you anticipate maturing by building something new in that environment? We've talked about doing your homework on each school, if not by visiting and talking to students there, then by finding alums and certainly scouring the websites. Are there specific classes you want to take? Are there clubs that you want to lead? Will you be able to start new things? Use these essays to show yourself that you can hit the ground running there, take advantage of their resources, and make a difference in the school community. When you finish each of these essays, you should feel certain that you want to go to school there. If you don't, then think about why the energy is falling flat. Use these essays to see if you feel a fit.

If you're applying to a particular major or preprofessional program, then the school may ask you about career goals. You already know your resume, and they'll see it in the application forms. These essays let you articulate the *motivations* for your significant elective courses, extracurriculars, and job choices. Think about *why* you have done the things you have done, what you learned, and why you moved on. Find the positives from each experience and discover how you have applied lessons learned in subsequent choices. If you have had a few random twists and turns, this is a great opportunity to consider and explain your reasoning for making changes. Don't be afraid to cite personal reasons for changes in your life (illness, family moved, or something else). Life happens! Be up-front about the facts and how such events influenced your thoughts and actions.

Be Authentic and Have Courage!

When it comes to writing these essays, own it and bring it. Own every part of yourself and bring it out onto the page. Leave nothing behind and let your authenticity pour out of you.

These essays are a chance to do your best. Don't let that scare you or put more pressure on you. Your best is your effortless, natural Self shining through. The work is only in removing the blocks of ego, attachment, aversion, and fear.

One of my favorite yoga teachers ends all of her classes by saying loudly and boldly, "Have courage." It shocked me a bit the first time I heard it. Now I look forward to it every time I take class with her. *Have courage.* How simple and powerful and just what we need to hear. When you face the page, *have courage.* Writing unlocks your soul like nothing else. Approach the essay-writing process with gratitude. It is a very concentrated crash course on self-study, a kind that many people never get. Soak it up and celebrate yourself through words only *you* could create.

✦ ✦ ✦

Since self-discovery through the essays is solo work, in chapter 4, we'll turn to look at who can help you out along the way in the overall application process, including recommenders and interviewers.

❖

Parents, Teachers, Coaches, Friends, Recommenders, and Even Interviewers

They Really *Can* Help You — If You Let Them

When people hear that I'm writing a book about applying to college, they are quick to share their own (or their child's or niece's or nephew's) application stories of stress, confusion, joy, and, all too often, heartbreak. It is a great privilege to hear these stories, as college admissions tales bring up very personal and vulnerable moments in people's lives.

At a wedding recently, I heard a beautiful story. I was there as a date, and I had never met the bride or groom before. It was the groom's second marriage; he already has a few children. It was a big day for him, you know, getting married and all. Yet upon meeting me and hearing about this book, he took time to talk about his daughter's impending interview for her first-choice school. She was understandably very nervous. She had applied early decision. Pressure was on. To prepare for her interview, she set about thinking of the right responses to probable questions, brainstorming the right way to describe herself, the right activities to mention, the right books to comment upon. Her wise dad told her to forget that rightness notion; she should talk about her quirky interests, share the weird books she loved, and be her fantastic self. He asked me if that was the right advice. Of course it was the right advice. In any situation, college interviews or otherwise, everyone should hear Dad say, "Be your quirky, fantastic self."

She got into the school. I'm sure her dad's advice helped because, as with the essays, it's a good move to be you in the interview. However, what transpired between the two of them around that stressful moment is much more important than interviews or college. It's about giving and getting love and support.

In this chapter, we'll take a look at potential "gurus," the people in your life who can give you props during this process. There's you for starters, as well as parents and siblings and friends, and teachers and coaches and such. And we'll hit on practical advice for dealing with recommenders (who ideally are part of your cheering section) and interviewers (who are actually on your side, as well).

Gurus to Your Rescue

Gu to the Ru. In Sanskrit, *gu* means darkness and *ru* means light. So a *guru* is one who helps you journey from darkness to light, from ignorance to knowledge. You suspected already that your boss at the frozen yogurt shop could lead you from darkness to light, no? But in fact, your gurus come in all shapes and sizes, from all times and places, even though you may not recognize them at first. Getting past your expectations and looking and listening with your heart can help you glean wisdom from surprisingly helpful souls. That said, there is also a traditional cast of characters floating around you during high school—parents, siblings, friends, teachers, coaches, bosses, guidance counselors, and so on. Keep in mind, though (as I've emphasized throughout this book so far), no one out there has the answers for you. What you are seeking is in *you* already. But the gurus in your life can give you important cues on when and why you might look within, just as you would do for others using your own guruness. We're all here to help a sister or a brother out.

How *You* Can Help Yourself

Let's start with your most obvious guru, which would be you—*you*. After all, you are in it for the long haul here with yourself. It would be good to start recognizing when you're not at the top of your game. Moreover, it will be very important to keep yourself humming along so that you're less prone to freaking out and losing perspective. With leaving high school and going to college, you're going to have much more independence in how you take care of yourself and balance your life.

Being your own guru means being aware. It's about coming back to the present moment and recognizing how you feel and what you need. When my brother Danny was a camp counselor and his campers got whiny, he would ask, "Are you hungry? Are you tired? Do you have to go to the bathroom?" No matter how old or evolved you are, you get cranky if you don't feel good inside. Basic self-care of body and then mind and spirit is fundamental to self-guruness—which is why I've devoted chapter 5 to dealing with stress and other stuff that gets in your way.

Moreover, college and adulthood brings tremendous independence in prioritizing parts of your life. Thus, it's a great opportunity to explore finding balance. This is the varsity of self-care. Usually, people don't start thinking about balance until they are working and doing the same thing all day (and maybe not liking it) and missing other aspects of their lives. One of the great things about high school and college is that you have work and school but also built-in opportunities for extracurricular activities and time with friends. Those are big things that we sadly lose once we start prioritizing work. If you can become aware of balance in your life now, you are going to have a head start as you become an independent adult in charge of your time. One common way to look over balance in your life is to use the Wheel of Life diagram, shown in Figure 4.1.

The sections in the Wheel of Life represent aspects of your life: school/work, money, health, family, friends/social, spiritual, dating/relationships, personal growth, fun/recreation, and physical environment. The categories are self-explanatory, with the exception of physical environment. This simply means the space where you live—like your room. Does it feel clean and peaceful, or is it cluttered and distracting? That kind of thing.

Imagine the center of the wheel is 0 and the outer edge is 10. Rank your level of satisfaction, with 0 being low and 10 high, by placing a dot inside the section for each category. Remember, you're ranking your *satisfaction*, how you *feel* about each area of your life. You're not ranking based on what you think you should be doing or what others think you should be doing. So let's say you're dating someone but you're not so into it. Then you might have a low number in that area, even though you're in a relationship. Similarly, you could have a 10 in that area, even if you're single,

FIGURE 4.1   **THE WHEEL OF LIFE**

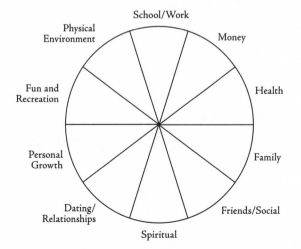

because you're good with that situation. Or let's say you're on a team, but it feels like work not fun. So fun and recreation might be low, even though you're technically involved with something in that area. Try hard to consider how you feel regarding each area of your life and whether you'd like the situation to be different.

Once you have your rankings, draw a line connecting the dots. The new perimeter represents the Wheel of Life for you and will give you a visual representation of how balanced your life is at this time.

How'd it go? Balance is something you can strive for, but it's important to remember that the wheel will look different at different times in your life. We all go through ebbs and flows in the chapters of our lives. Like right now, when your life is very much about school and working like crazy on your applications, you might not be paying that much attention to dating or spirituality. Watch out for your inner achievement ogre that's telling you that success means 10s across the board. There's no success or failure with this; it's a diagnostic tool. Be honest with yourself and respect that there are timelines for each area of your life. Sometimes we want to be places where we just aren't yet. The karmic viewpoint, which we'll discuss more deeply in the next chapter, would be to look at that area of life and see what lessons you could be learning, then have faith that you'll move forward when you're ready to change your thoughts and behavior. The Wheel of Life is simply giving you information about yourself and how you feel.

At the base of self-care is loving and respecting yourself. Okay, now that really sounds like your kindergarten teacher, but that teacher was on to something! Remember, what the world really needs is you to be your highest self. Corny as it sounds, by truly loving yourself from outside in and inside out, you will be your best. You will be more of your Self—your most peaceful, compassionate, generous, inspiring, effective, impactful, stunning, and radiant you.

Parents: They're Trying!

When I was teaching third grade, I had my students make Mother's Day cards for their moms or grandmas or whatever woman was doing the hard work of raising them. One of my students, Eric, made a gorgeous card, all hearts and rainbows. Inside, he intended to write, "Mom, you are the BEST!" Unfortunately, Eric's sounding-out skills were still coming along, so his beautiful card included this message: "Mom, you are the BEAST!" Wow. I let it go home just like that.

We've all felt at some point that our parents are the best *and* the beast. That's the nature of the parent-child tango. Thus far, I've given parents a bum rap by shutting them out of the essay-writing process. But if you're lucky, you have parents who want to be involved in this college application work and with your life in general, so try not to shut them out of everything. Key gurus are people who have more experience, and even if your parents haven't been to college, they do know more than a thing or two about life and you.

Here is the deal with parents—they just want you to be

happy. I swear. Yet I know how annoying that sounds when you're annoyed with them. (And this never ends: recently, over dinner with a friend, I was kvetching about something my parents did/said/thought; he told me that they just want me to be happy, and I almost threw my salad at him. And I'm a lot older than you are!) The thing is, your parents are on their own life path. They know what made *them* happy or what they think would have made them happy. On top of that, they also want you to have a better life than they did in whatever terms are meaningful to them. So their ambitions for you are wrapped up in their own ambitions, fulfilled or otherwise. It's a complicated situation in some ways, and in others ways, it's very simple. Your parents love you more than you can possibly imagine until maybe you have your own kids. They want you to be happy. They want you to feel fulfilled and successful. They may trip up, in your mind, on how they help you out with this. So be it. They are human and fallible, and that's just the way things go.

Plus, if you think you're stressed and confused during this application time, your parents may be even worse off. They want to protect you, but they also want to respect your boundaries. They want to help, but they have no control over what you're going through. On top of that, they are about to lose you when you go off to college. You may not realize this, but you are a great time! Even when you and your parents are fighting, you are the best thing that's ever happened to them. I see it with my friends who are new parents and with my brother and my nephew; there is nothing more spectacular, it seems, than having a kid. So they are bumming hard that you're going to leave them. This is especially true if you're the youngest in your family and your folks are facing a totally new life with you gone.

After I said good-bye to my parents, which was for sure sad and scary for me, I bopped down the hall of my freshman dorm at Northwestern introducing myself to people. I learned later that my parents collapsed on each other in the stairwell, weeping. I got to go to a dorm barbecue with my new buddies. They had to drive back to Maryland worried and heartbroken. The dorm barbecue is the way better deal. This does not mean you need to take care of your parents—not at all! That is so *not* your job. They need to do that for themselves. It just means you may have to be patient with them as they fumble during this year or so of your life. They want you to be an independent, thriving adult, yet they aren't quite sure how to help you with that. It's a rough time for you and for them. Best if all parties cut each other some slack.

For all of their fumbles and all of your issues with them, there a zillion areas where your parents can be life-saving gurus. We'll start with a fun one. Your parents can be a huge resource in helping you recognize your gifts. (Remember your gifts? It's good to know what these are when you're filling out college applications and writing those essays, and if you've forgotten this already, see chapters 2 and 3.) They knew you when you were little and saw what you loved to do. They may not have had the time, resources, or knowledge to help you pursue such things, but they can help you think about what came really easily for you and what made you super happy back before you started thinking too much. One applicant's mom was the one who reminded him that he has always been a performer; it was his calling to be on stage somewhere, somehow. Your parents may have even been the ones who stopped you from doing such things because they didn't think they were practical, like the applicant whose mom made her stop dancing to do more "college-oriented" activities, like high-jumping. Again, the mom was just trying to help her daughter out. Forgive your parents for caring, even if they shut you down. Either way, try to get them to tell you what you were like when you were little. One of the ways you may be getting stressed or stuck during this process, and in life in general, is that you aren't doing things in line with your gifts. So getting information from your parents on your natural gifts is really helpful.

One of the big ways in which your parents can be great gurus is by helping you see when you are stuck, stressed, or just not dealing well. Granted, this is when your parents drive you freaking nuts. We'll talk through specific obstacles that come up in chapter 5, but for now, just keep in mind that your parents will often be the ones to alert you that you're in one of those places—not getting things done, being bored, acting hastily, etc. When your parents are bugging you about how you're behaving, it's legit for you to be irritated up to your eyeballs with them. But try to hear what they are noticing about your behavior because there are important clues in there. Without giving them the satisfaction of showing them that you are listening, you can still hear what they are saying and use it to help move yourself along to a place where you'll feel better and be more productive.

Of course, your parents are also super-duper gurus because they love you to bits. You're about to enter a much sweeter parent time once you leave for school. Suddenly, you do want to talk to your mom about your breakup and maybe heed your dad's advice on taking econ. Or maybe your dad is the relationship guru, and your mom knows why chemistry is a good time. A little space is huge for this relationship. As you get older, they will see how wise you are, and you will see that they aren't total morons. Until then, as you go through this application process and everything else, hopefully your parents will tell you that you are awesome and remind you just to be yourself, because that's the best advice they can give you. If not, know that's what they want to do but it's not so easy to get the parenting thing just right, whereas we all know being the perfect child comes naturally. Ha!

Siblings: Experience and Wisdom

Whether they are older or younger, siblings can be valuable in passing on some life (and application lessons), as well as helping you see yourself more clearly, understand where you've come from, and hopefully celebrate where you're going. Depending on your relationship with them, they can be a huge help during this process. And let's face it: every family is strange, so when you need to get a witness to the weirdness that is your family life and your parents, siblings can be your go-to gurus.

One of the benefits of being the youngest is that you get to watch your older siblings give life a go first. If you pay attention, you can learn key high school lessons—do find a sport you love, don't leave your massive paper until Sunday night after dinner, do explore your artistic side, don't sneak drinks at your aunt's wedding and throw up in front of your entire family in the car on the way home.

With the college app game, your older siblings can be a big help, if only because you get to watch them go through it. The process seems a bit more doable if someone in your house has indeed done it. You can lean on your older sibling for advice, depending on what your relationship is like, or you can just watch and learn. Many applicants watch their siblings tackle the essays for better or worse. I vaguely remember my brother Danny saying one night, "If you want to know what a nervous breakdown looks like, this is it!" Ironic, since he became the writing coach who best chilled me out during my college essays, college thesis, and even this book.

Other applicants had their school choices expanded by watching their siblings, like the applicant who first considered applying to more competitive schools after watching his brother get into Columbia. So many younger siblings I've spoken to apply and even go to the same colleges as their big brothers and sisters. "I mostly chose Haverford because my big sister was there and I was scared to death to go to college on my own," said one. I applied to Bowdoin when I was a senior and again as a transfer, though Danny was long graduated by then, because it felt familiar and welcoming. Or the opposite is true: one guy wasn't too excited about applying to Yale because his older brother was there and they had a rocky relationship.

Even if your relationship isn't the best right now, older siblings can be important gurus down the line when it comes to your gifts and callings. Like your parents, they have known you your whole life. Depending on how much they've been around and your age range, they may know you pretty well. They are primed and ready to help you remember who you were at a younger age in terms of gifts exploration. They can help you think through choices about schools, majors, and jobs because they faced it all first. One little sister followed her brother through undergrad, banking, and then business school. On the flip side, many little siblings chose professions that were the opposite of those of older siblings; one girl didn't go the law school route because her brother hated it. Older siblings can also keep you in check and encourage you better than parents at times, because their aspirations aren't wrapped up in your choices. Mostly though, they can make the world seem safer and better just because they are out there.

Younger siblings ... I am one so I'm not sure how we help other than being God's gift of joy and perfection to the family. Ha ha. I'm certain we're a pain in the buttress during the college process. My shy older brother Danny tried to hang in the back of his college tours while I, a fifth grader, practically tackled the Amherst tour guide out of enthusiasm over seeing who even knows what (the student union?) and laughed hysterically when he stepped in dog-doo in front of the Yale dorms. I tagged along with my parents to Mike's parents weekends at the University of Vermont and hijacked outings to shop for earthy-crunchy college girl sweaters in earthy-crunchy Burlington. On behalf of all annoying, self-absorbed, and spoiled younger siblings, I apologize to you older ones. However, the older siblings I've worked with note that they've gained a bit of confidence from showing younger siblings the ropes. So in our cluelessness, younger siblings can help you see how much you know about school and life. Also younger siblings can add some lightness to your life when they aren't driving you insane. As I mentioned when writing about gifts in chapter 2, my nephew is a great reminder of how to follow interests and passions. Let your younger siblings be gurus to you in this way. Let them keep you connected to that excellent younger life force inside you. And when they are bugging, know that they don't understand what you're going through. Remember how much they admire you and love you and will want your help when it's their turn.

Friends: You Can Get By with a Little Help From Them

You already know that your friends are the bomb. Only they truly understand what you're going through because they are going through it themselves. They will keep you laughing and sane, and that perspective is a true guru gift. Your friends can also help you see the truth and give you great advice. The students that I mentor through the nonprofit are huge gurus for each other. They help each other choose schools: "Is Cornell really right for you?" "You would *love* Brown!" "You should definitely check out Emory." "Here, take my view book on Colgate." They share SAT prep materials and remind each other of important sign-up dates for tests. They help each other brainstorm essay topics: "You've got to write about your drama club." "Tell them how important authenticity is to you." "Tell them that you walk around serenading classrooms at school." They also talk each other down when the stress hits: "Don't worry. Your recommender will get the rec in on time." "You've studied enough—just go in and take the test." Let your friends be your coaches and do the same for them.

Most important, your friends see how amazing you are, just as you see that in them. So make it a point to remind each other of your awesomeness when your confidence is faltering. After high school, you are going to make great friends at college, work, graduate school, and all over the place. But there's nothing quite like the relationships with the people who knew you at 7 and 17. If they don't already, your high school friends will come to feel like family down the line because they know where you come from. Cherish them, champion them, and let them do the same for you now and forever.

Mentors: Find Them

There are a bunch of authority figure adults floating through your life right now. Let's be honest. Some of them are great. Some of them, not so much. You're a perceptive person and will know which ones can help you out. For the purposes of the guru search, the point is that it's on *you* to make the good eggs into mentors. They can give you advice around college or life in general with a different take than your parents. When you're down, they can pep-talk you back into the game. However, it can be tough to initiate a mentor type relationship with a teacher or coach. Sometimes we feel shy and don't want to bother an adult with extra questions or take up time. Try to get over this. Hopefully, teachers, coaches, and guidance counselors have gone into those jobs because they want to help kids. So let them.

Let's start with the obvious college application guru — the college or guidance counselor. Ideally, your school has a counselor you can trust and ask for advice. I went to a huge public school, so I didn't know our guidance counselor well. I had the mandatory meeting with her, and she made sure I had a list that included safety schools, probables, and reaches. She was obviously a busy woman. I should have taken some responsibility and asked her for help on how to explain my weak freshman year grades to colleges. When schools see an inconsistency in your record, they just want to understand what happened. Your college counselor can help you determine the best ways to address parts of your application that seem weak or need further explanation. Take responsibility to let him or her know what you need. Similarly, tell your counselor which schools are most important to you. One friend applied to Boston College, her first choice, and a bunch of small New England liberal arts schools much like her small liberal private high school. Boston College was the only school she didn't get into. When she later told the guidance counselor it had been her first choice, the counselor was surprised. She could have have helped my friend more with that application, but she assumed my friend wanted a small New England liberal arts school based on the rest of her choices. Communicate, people! Counselors can't help you unless they know what you want.

At the same time, remember that your guidance counselor is also thinking about people other than you; he or she has to consider your high school as a whole. So the counselor's advice needs to be taken with a grain of salt. One friend who went to a fancy East Coast boarding school was discouraged from applying to Harvard by his guidance counselor. He was applying to Yale, so his profile wasn't the issue. He said she was controlling the numbers of who applied where; they couldn't have everyone apply to Harvard because they needed to keep the fancy school's acceptance ratios desirable. To this I say, "Hell no!" Definitely take advice from experienced people who might know if you're a good fit somewhere. But in the end, it's your life. So if you want to apply somewhere, then apply there. Done and done.

Your teachers can help you out in many ways, from giving general advice to reading over essays to writing recommendations. Having been a teacher, I think the best part of the job is watching your students grow up and gain confidence. It's great to see them master multiplication, and I'm sure watching you knock your history exam out of the park is gratifying. But none of it tops seeing you become sure of yourself. You will know which teachers are in your corner; you'll just click with them and feel inspired in their classes. One applicant had an English teacher who really pushed her. He suggested that she turn an essay she'd written for his class into an application essay; he even read many drafts to help her get it right. Also, don't forget your teachers from before senior year. They can be great mentors because they have known you for a while. One applicant stayed really close with his sophomore year English teacher and got lots of college advice from him. The teacher even remembered one of the applicant's great essays and suggested reworking it for college applications. You'll recognize the teachers who could be mentors because you feel comfortable talking to them and maybe they start asking you about where you're thinking of applying to school.

But even adults can be shy, so you may have to take the initiative to talk. You can start by asking them about their college experience; people love to talk about themselves. Ask questions, and then they will do the same. Not all of them need to become recommenders, and we'll talk about choosing folks for that distinction next. Instead, this is about building a support staff of mentors.

There are also the great teachers who sponsor your clubs or coach your teams, or maybe your school uses outside professionals for these roles. Either way, these folks will get to know you outside of the classroom; they'll see you using your gifts and following your bliss in many ways. They can be hugely helpful in the mentor role because you're not getting graded by them. You'll also probably have casual conversations with them about what's next in your life; it won't be all business as it can be with classroom teachers. Again, though, the initiative may be on you to let them help you. But they too want to help you in as many ways as possible with realizing your college dreams. One of my friends ended up at Harvard thanks to her tennis coach. He asked her where she was applying. Duke, Washington University, Michigan, University of North Carolina, SUNY–Binghamton. He asked why there weren't any Ivies on the list. She said that at $65 an application, she couldn't afford to apply, especially if it was wasted on a rejection. He said he'd pay for applications to four Ivy League schools and if she went to one, then she had to get him a sweatshirt from the school. She took him up on the offer and applied to Harvard, Brown, Dartmouth, and Columbia. She got into all of them and went to Harvard. I'm assuming he got his sweatshirt.

One quick note is that you are looking for mentors who build your self-esteem and promote teamwork. The ones who make you feel insecure and competitive with your classmates aren't worth your time. Never let adults, or anyone, make you feel bad about yourself. They are struggling with their own sad issues. Let them go and do not to take their garbage personally. It's their garbage. They shouldn't take it out on you. One guy I know struggled with a coach who, for whatever jacked-up personal reasons, didn't do his part helping his athletes get recruited by colleges. A bunch of guys on the team didn't get the scholarships or opportunities at colleges they could have gotten had the coach supported them more. If you are experiencing something like that, try to let go of the anger towards the coach and instead push into overdrive to find a solution yourself. The point is to pay attention to who can help you, let go of those who can't or won't, and stay in forward motion.

If you have a job or internship outside of school, your boss or manager could be a mentor, as well. It depends on the nature of the job and their experience, of course, as to whether they can help you think about college. Even without college experience, a boss may serve in the guru capacity. These characters are often some of the best we have in our worlds. I've seen applicants get great advice from senior-level business and political types as well as managers at Starbucks. Cast a wide net in looking for the people who can give you advice and help you think about things just a wee bit deeper.

You can also find mentors through professional organizations. As I've mentioned, I'm a mentor to high school seniors through a nonprofit in New York. We talk about college applications, but we also just hang out and talk about life. It's one of the aspects of my life for which I am most grateful. We have such a great time, and I learn a ton from them. You don't realize how wise and mature you are, or hopefully you do. It is a gift for people to know you. So if you'd like to find a mentor, ask your guidance counselor, teachers, principal, or parents to help you find opportunities, or go online to see if any organizations near you facilitate that type of thing.

Recommenders: Let Them Do Their Jobs

Some of these mentors will become your recommenders for college. The lucky ones! Writing your recommendations is an honor and a big responsibility. Choose people who are worthy of this role. One girl chose her AP history teacher who was young and fun. It had been a small, special class that had even taken a trip from their hometown of New Orleans to New York City. She felt a special connection with this teacher and that she'd done her best in this class. However, your recommender may not be the teacher who gave you the best grades. One friend asked the teacher who pushed her the hardest. She wasn't the teacher's favorite, nor did she get her highest grades in at class, but she'd worked incredibly hard and learned a lot. She felt she'd earned that teacher's respect.

Sometimes your recommender isn't a teacher. One applicant chose her cross-country coach. She wasn't the star of the team; in fact, she wasn't a natural athlete and had to push herself hard to keep up. This coach could speak to her commitment and character, which mattered a lot more to colleges than her times. One girl asked the principal of her high school. She happened to have a good relationship with him because she was really involved in extracurriculars and he went to every play, sporting event, etc. Her grades weren't her strongest point, and he could talk about her character and what she brought to the school community. He could say that her slightly lower GPA wasn't because she didn't try hard. Quite the contrary! She was doing an amazing job of balancing all of her activities, and she made conscious choices to enrich her life and develop into a school leader. She felt he understood what she was about and what was most important to her. Indeed, that should be most important. Pick the person who knows you well.

A good recommendation is one that can give lots of fun, specific details about your personality, passions, sense of humor, and general coolness. When I was director of admissions at Teach For

America, a great rec was one that made me think, "Ooh, I can't wait to meet this candidate!" Strong recommendations are heartfelt and enthusiastic. Granted in the above example, this heartfelt recommendation came from the principal. However, the girl didn't choose him because he was the principal. This comes up more with graduate school, but please do not make the mistake of picking someone who is "important" or an alum of your school of choice over someone who knows you better. Go for the person who can really talk about you.

Ideally, your recommenders know you well and are very invested in your candidacy. So try to find true mentors. This is why it helps to start developing mentor relationships as soon as possible. Then the recommenders will know about your hopes, dreams, and breadth of interests beyond just your classroom performance, artistic talents, or athletic abilities. You also want to look for recommenders who can express their thoughts about you with vibrancy and clarity. Go with that idea of following the energy: Which mentors make you feel more alive and intelligent? Those people would make good recommenders.

Your school probably has some guidelines on how the recommendations are submitted. Ask your guidance counselor or teachers about this. It's polite to give your recommenders at least a month to write the recommendations. Even better, give them more time to think about what they'll write. If you aren't sure of your school choices, you can still ask them early in the fall. That way they can begin brainstorming great examples and then write once you've nailed down your school list. Definitely take the time to have a conversation with them about why you think they could be great recommenders; you can discuss what you want from college and maybe even an example or two of your skills, interests, and personality.

As much as you want to help your recommenders, however, please don't try to control the rec. It's helpful for schools to get a fresh take on you from someone else. Let your recommenders do their job. Your role is simply to help them see who you are beyond just your academic capacity and to see what's important to you in life.

Interviewers: All You Can Do Is Be Yourself

What is not to love about the interview? You get to talk about yourself for an hour, and you don't have to pay someone $150 to listen. Shocking as this may sound, your interviewers also want the best for you, and they can be essential gurus. First things first, they want you to feel comfortable and open during your conversation. One friend remembers that she wanted to appear serious and intellectual to her Harvard alum interviewer. This was made all the more difficult because my friend had an enormous crush on this woman's son. Fortunately, the interviewer was a really cool woman who made it comfortable and easy for my friend to talk about things in which she was genuinely interested. For the record, one of these things was *Elle* magazine. Be yourself. People at Ivy League schools do read *Elle*.

Having served as an alumni interviewer for Stanford and having interviewed a massive number of Teach For America applicants, I can tell you that a good interview is one where the candidate is loose, natural, and reflective. One friend remembers wearing a plaid skirt, cardigan sweater, and penny loafers to her Dartmouth interview (not her usual style) so that she could look the part, but she was sure to be herself and stay really honest even if she was in costume. She got in, so that worked out. But please don't feel you need to wear a costume or be a character. Try to relax; see it as a conversation and enjoy yourself.

As with every step in this college application process, you can learn a lot about yourself during the interview. Think about lessons learned from experiences and share all the different aspects of you. Speaking your mind, sharing your past, and articulating your dreams is powerful stuff. Rarely do we say such things out loud. When you walk out of your interview, you want to have learned about yourself. If you have, then the interviewer has learned about you, as well.

So keep in mind the wise dad's advice from the start of the chapter: just be you. You are not trying to sell something. Also, remember that there's no "right" answer to think of on the spot. Of course, it's a good idea to read over your application essays and think about why you want to go to each school before you go into your interviews. Your reasons for wanting to go to Reed are *your* reasons; take this opportunity to explore them again. You may also want to practice talking to yourself in front of a mirror so you get used to hearing yourself discuss these ideas out loud. Remember that you'll be asked the basics—why this school—but be open to answering questions about your life and interests.

Interviewers also have guru potential because here you have either an alum or a staff member of the school with firsthand knowledge. Go ahead and ask about these people's experiences, and take some mental notes on whether what they are saying feels like what you want to hear about your future college. Alums love to talk about their schools, especially alums who are serving as interviewers. You can find out about their time there and what they loved most and what surprised them—whatever you want to know. You will also get a general feel for the schools. One friend who really wanted to go to Trinity did not at all feel a fit with her interviewer. She felt as though she were trying to make the interviewer like her, but they just had very different personalities. However, she got along great with the Lehigh interviewer who was an older man; she felt as though she could have talked to him for hours. She was sad when Trinity rejected her, but Lehigh turned out to be just the right school for her. Looking back, she wished she'd appreciated the signs that came out during the interviews.

Or maybe the lack of interview is an indication of a fit or not. One girl really wanted an interview for University of Michigan, but she didn't have one. She got in anyway and went there, but she always wondered if she would have liked a smaller school with a more personal feel. Looking back, that desire for a more personal experience began when she wasn't interviewed before being accepted. All of that said, maybe my friend and the Trinity woman just didn't get along. And remember way back to chapter

1, you can determine through your own initiative how personal your academic experience feels, no matter what size the school is. The point is that both of these people had gut feelings around their interviews that were previews to their general experiences with the schools.

So keep paying attention. Maybe you're fortunate enough to interview with an admissions committee member. If so, you can get that person's thoughts on what the students say about certain aspects of the school, how it's changing, and what might surprise you about it. Don't miss this opportunity to do more research.

Finally, one of the most important reasons just to be you at the interview is that's the only thing you can control. In fact, of all of the aspects of the application process, this is the one where you have the least amount of control. Interviewers will be interviewers, and you never know what's going to happen or who you're going to get, as in these two examples.

First, one girl was supposed to meet with a Columbia alum in downtown Portland at a Starbucks. Her dad drove her there and she sat in Starbucks, waiting and waiting. Then she realized there were four Starbucks on that street, so she sent her poor dad running around to try to hunt the guy down (while she waited at the original post). Her dad finally found him at the Peet's Coffee a few blocks away; he'd gotten Peet's confused with Starbucks. Argh! She said it was all downhill from there. She was convinced she'd blown her chance at Columbia by unknowingly going to the wrong coffee place—her confidence was shot, she kept apologizing, and almost cried. We all feel her pain. She didn't get into Columbia, though she doesn't blame the coffee shop snafu. She got really wrapped up in being who Columbia wanted, which she thought was more academic and serious than she was. We know now that trying to be someone other than herself was her only real mistake! Ironically, six years later, she got into Columbia for grad school and turned it down because she didn't think it was the right fit for her, a move that stunned (and pleased) her inner 18-year-old!

This next interview example is from a business school candidate, but it bears mentioning because it's so over-the-top crazy. I'd prepped with this really nice guy for his Stanford interview. He was so ready, and he couldn't wait to articulate all of the reasons he was a great fit for Stanford. He went down to the investment bank where a senior partner would be interviewing him. The applicant walked in, and the interviewer said, "Hey, thanks for coming down here. Your resume's great. I've got a good track record of my interviewees getting in. So I'll give you a good write-up. Have a great day." That was it. That was the interview. There was no interview! The poor applicant was so weirded out. He had *no* control over what was going to happen, and he was bummed to miss the chance to discuss Stanford with another alum. He got in (so the interviewer's good track record continues), though I doubt the interview write-up was the highlight of his application.

Look, you never know what's going to go down with the interviewer. Hopefully, you'll make a good connection, get some guru wisdom on the school, and have a good time. All you can do is be yourself.

Gurus Go On and On

Of course, this is just the beginning of the gurus at your side. So many people will be ready to take the field for you when you need them over the course of your life. You know how much you love to help other people? They feel that way about you, too! It's one of our greatest gifts as humans to be able to support each other. Let yourself turn to those around you. Let yourself be open to their care and their questions and their cheerleading. We all need it because this practice of life thing is not a smooth ride.

✦ ✦ ✦

Now that you're thinking about who's on your side, let's get into some of the common obstacles we all face as we make our way.

CHAPTER 5

❖

Overcoming Obstacles

Bust through Stress, Exhaustion, Boredom, and Frustration; Learn Your Lessons and Keep the Faith

Applying to schools can bring on massive stress. There's so much work on top of everything else you've got going on. Perhaps there's tons of pressure, either self-imposed or otherwise. Mostly, though, there seems to be the sense that it's a make-it-or-break-it moment in your life. In the countless talks I've had with people who are anywhere from 2 to 42 years past this application process, they all had the same wish — that someone had told them it's going to be okay. So here goes…

It's going to be okay.

I didn't really expect that to take away all the stress, but it was worth a shot. Look, even if you are focusing on the present, letting go of the outcomes and releasing attachments, discovering your Self and keeping the faith, and learning your lessons and finding your bliss, there are bound to be a few moments of epic freaking out. 'Tis the nature of the college application beast. It gets to us sometimes. And we crack.

This is a chapter dedicated to the freak-outs in your life now and forever more. For no matter how much perspective we have, there are times when we all need someone to grab us by the lapels and scream, "You must chill. You must chill." So this chapter is about learning how to chill—to care of yourself, body, mind, and spirit, as you move into adulthood. It's about recognizing when you're stressed and stuck and helping to move yourself along. And it's about the importance of letting others help you, too.

We'll look at some of the common pitfalls that come up for all of us on our life journeys, applying to college included. Sometimes stress looks just the way you think it will: tension and exhaustion. But sometimes the tough moments of your life look a little different. You might get resistant and lethargic, even bored. Other times, you might act with haste, being sloppy and avoiding real work. You can get stuck and prevent yourself from moving forward. And there's bound to be a time of thinking you know it all, and then maybe seeing there's much more work to do be done. Obstacles on your path will appear in different ways at different times in your life, so this chapter will show how to explore these times and how to address them.

At a base level, these blocks are born in the four demons we discussed in chapter 3, which often get in our way—ego, attachment, aversion, and fear—but they manifest in different ways. Sometimes we don't recognize them as stress or obstacles or blocks and think blah-ness or stuck-ness or tired-ness is just the way life is.

But that's *not* the way life has to be. You have the power and spirit to make your life big, beautiful, and rich with learning and progress—all the time. These obstacles are great opportunities to see when you've steered off course and aren't feeling fulfilled or inspired. Usually, they mean you can take in some lessons about the direction you're headed or how you're getting there. The tough moments kick you in the boo-tay and get you back in forward motion. Don't settle for some subpar, stressed-out, small existence.

Over the course of the college application process, obstacles can rear their ugly heads around anything and everything: studying for and taking the SATs, selecting which schools to apply to, writing essays, getting homework done, filling out applications, organizing supplementary materials, getting in touch with coaches, finding recommenders, scheduling interviews, preparing for interviews, waiting to hear from schools, making the decision, and even getting ready to go to school. As this chapter describes the different obstacles that can get in your way, think about where these behaviors or issues might be showing up in *your* life right now.

Stress and Exhaustion: You Must Chill

The real freak show kicks in junior year. There's just something in the air when junior year starts, and it snowballs into madness by senior fall. SAT prep starts. Grades matter more. People start asking where you'll apply. It's all exhausting. I vividly remember walking through crowded, noisy E hall of my high school during senior fall and thinking, "I am so tired. I could lie down right here and fall asleep with people stepping over me." And then at night, I'd lie in bed wide-awake while my monkey mind refereed a past-future ping-pong match.

You're tired. You're wired. You feel like garbage. And your exhaustion is most likely caused by all the stress you're feeling. Physical stress is pretty easy to recognize, and it does a huge number on our bodies. Huge. One simple but profound fact: you have one body to take you through life. The knees, stomach, lungs, and eyes you've got right now are the same ones you had when you were a baby and will have for the rest of this here life. Your body remembers what you've been through and reflects what you're going through now. As I mentioned in chapter 1 on chakras and energy, your body shows your emotional/mental state and vice versa.

So when you're in a time of stress—like when you're writing essays and trying to get great grades and figuring out where you want to go to school and waiting to hear from schools—you want to be good to your body. Even if your mind is going nutso, being nice to your body will decrease the effects of the stress. Plus, your well-cared-for body will help your mind chill out. Moreover, you'll prevent today's inevitable stress from doing a number on your long-term health. The advice on this front is pretty basic. Eat. Sleep. Move. Breathe.

You Need to Eat—and Not Just Junk Food

High school is a great time to practice feeding yourself well. If you can start taking care of yourself now, you'll see how good you feel and then perhaps do slightly less damage while you're applying to college and once you get there—because college is a buffet, literally, of nonsense on the eating front. My mom commented once that when my brothers first returned from college, they looked as though all they'd been eating was potatoes. Mmm, potatoes. At Northwestern, we fell into an all-cereal routine. I have no idea if Cracklin' Oat Bran still exists, but don't, I repeat *do not*, get started on that addiction. There's a reason "crack" is in the name of that stuff. During my late-night thesis-writing hours at Harvard, my fuel of choice was M&M's and Coke (not diet, the real stuff—bring it on). I don't like coffee, and you only get so much kick from hot cocoa. I got my first cavities then along with extra pounds and junkie shakes. But hey, who knows, maybe you run well on all M&M's all the time. Maybe you don't.

The point is that what you put into your body really will change how you feel. And you can start paying attention to that now. That said, there will be times for fabulous full-body abuse on the food front, so don't deny yourself the pleasure that is pizza debrief with friends at 3:00 AM after being out. But overall, when you're dealing with exams and essays and extracurricular activities and generally getting stuff done now and at college, feeding your-self well helps big-time. It's hard for your spirit to shine through a layer of potato chips.

You Also Need to Sleep

You know what else feels awesome? Sleeping. It rocks. We barely slept during high school, and maybe you're up to the same tricks. School starts at like 5:00 AM right? You're fighting a losing battle. You'll probably sleep more during college just because your class schedule won't feel like the all-day forced march of high school. Plus, there will be all those hours you log facedown in your book in the library. Oh, the poor guy that farted (big-time) whilst snoozing in one of the comfy red leather chairs in Harvard's Lamont library on a snowy Monday night. He woke up everybody but himself thankfully; no one should know they've done that.

Back to the point, college application season may be the most sleep-challenged time in your near future. You may desire that nap on the floor of your school between classes. As with the food thing, experiment and pay attention to how you feel when you get certain amounts of sleep. Try to get a bit more than you think you need. Your brain, essays, and homework will thank you for it. And who wants to sleepwalk through high school?

Don't Forget to Exercise Your Body While You're Focused on Your Brain

Okay, even if you go with the three-hours-of-sleep-Cracklin'-Oat-Bran lifestyle, do try to shake what your mama gave you. Run, row,

swim, spin, climb, kick, dance, or do yoga. Find some way to sweat
and breathe and let it all out. The food, the sleep, those soapboxes
can float on by, but I will hop up on the exercise one. Working
out in whatever form you choose will change your life.

As a yoga teacher, I watch this happen to people every day
over and over again. It can be kind of tricky to inhabit your own
body, as silly as that sounds. We all have issues with what we got
in the genetic lottery. But moving your body helps you connect
with it and live in it. You'll start sensing what it wants and what
it's telling you. You'll grow to appreciate it, feed it well, and give
it rest. Plus, it's much easier to tap into the deep wisdom of the
heart and gut when you feel these parts of yourself. Not to mention the endorphin-happy rush from working out. If there's one
thing that's like magic in the self-care department, it's this one.
Move it or lose it.

Find Some Truly Quiet Time

Once you're done moving your body … stop. We also need stillness
and quiet to replenish our bodies, minds, and spirits. Just as you
pay attention to what you feed your body, you can keep tabs on
what you're feeding your mind—through TV, movies, Internet,
music. All of that stuff is food in a way. Try getting conscious
of how what you're doing, watching, reading, and hearing affects
your body and mind. That awareness will help you discover what
makes you feel peaceful and what makes you feel crazy.

Also, if you can, try to find some time every day to get quiet.
Even just taking three deep conscious breaths from time to time

can do wonders on the chilling-out front. Can you sit for three minutes, maybe right when you wake up? Simply hear and feel your breath coming in and out, as mentioned in chapter 1. It can also help to find books or places that inspire this quiet space in your life. Your spirit, your soul, your Self flourishes in this stillness. Let yourself feel that peace you're looking for inside. Again, it only takes a couple of breaths and you're right there with your Self.

Resistance: Step Up and Beat It Down

What is grosser than sitting down to write admissions essays? Even with everything I suggested in chapter 3 — the journaling practice and lure of self-discovery and channeling your writer persona — sitting down to write is just plain hard. We've all felt this resistance across our lives, and it's a big obstacle with college applications.

Resistance takes on different forms:

+ There's the pure *procrastination* road: you're too busy with homework, soccer practice, or reorganizing your desk to actually start working on applications.

+ *Indecision* is also appealing: you're not sure where you want to apply, not sure what to write about.

+ You can also do the *ambivalence* dance: Should you even be going to school right now? Is college for you?

- Then there's just plain *lethargy*: maybe you're watching TV, emailing, hanging around, or just too tired to do anything.

No matter what form it takes—procrastination, indecision, ambivalence, lethargy—it's our old friend *fear* driving your resistance bus. It's about fear of the unknown, fear of shedding your old life, fear of moving forward, fear of making a big change, fear of whether you can step up, fear of whether you're good enough. It makes perfect sense. Change means leaving behind safety, whether it's your comfortable addictive patterns or easy youthful immaturity or an old story about who you are and what you're capable of. Stepping into a bigger version of yourself and letting more of your spirit come forward is risky and scary. And applying to college asks you to put yourself out there. Yet you'll see this resistance come up again and again in relationships, sports, your professional career, or anytime you're unsure about taking things to the next level.

Often, though, you don't see resistance in yourself or want to admit what's behind it. You might feel bummed because you're indecisive or tired, or you might just feel comfortable not changing or taking action. Deep down, though, you know you're holding back, letting something you really want slip away, resisting growing into a bigger, brighter you. Sometimes a parent, friend, significant other, or teacher notices that you're backing down from something or getting lazy. When they call you on it, you might get annoyed—especially if you quickly see that they are right on.

You can focus on your irritation with them, or you can consider what they are saying and maybe take action.

For example, my little nephew has mastered bike riding. Helmet on, he's ready to go—until it gets kinda hard. We were on a bike ride once with rolling hills that were tough on his little-boy body. As we got to a big hill, he started whining about his shorts, stopping to fix his helmet, hanging back from the rest of us. As his (annoying) yoga Auntie KK, I told him that the cure to exhaustion is not rest but effort. (Seriously, I stun myself with how annoying I can be.) Just focus on pumping your legs, stand up and see what that does for you, concentrate on pushing the pedals down... After some understandable grumbling, he went for it. He got focused, which is really cute on a seven-year-old's face. He started kicking some butt, got through the hill, and then was a chipper dude. He was scared that he couldn't bike up the hill. But he could. And you can, too.

When you are facing resistance, it is time to answer the call! You're backing down in the face of fear. No biggie. That's what happens on the brink of great change. When you meet your edge, you freak. It may seem as though you're not capable of what's on the other side. You are. Or maybe you don't think you deserve the sweetness of change. You do. If you step up to that edge and work there, you will meet with yummy transformation.

Answering the call is about restating your intentions. Get clear about what you want, what lessons you're learning, where you want to go. It can help to do this formally. Sit and think about what's coming for you. Journal about your goals. Maybe even create a ceremony for yourself, whether it's just stating out loud what you want, lighting a candle, shouting it from a rooftop, or whispering it to a tree. Translating your intentions into a moment or symbol can make them more powerful, real, and possible. It's easier to focus when you know what you're working towards. Once you are clear about the hill that's in front of you, pump the pedals more. Answer resistance with effort. Fear of change does not stand a chance over faith in yourself.

Boredom: What 'Chu Want?

I was reeeaaalllly bored during most classes at business school. Totally my fault. I was at freaking Stanford. The professors rocked. My classmates were all Smartie McFacscinating. But to me, most classes felt like watching paint dry. It was Charlie Brown in school... wha, whaaa, wha, whaaa, wha. Not like everyone there was whooping it up during accounting. Some things are just a bit boring. (No offense, accountants: you've been blessed with an interest in accounting to save us all.) But during classes or while reading or studying for tests, I was dying. The boredom continued into my consulting and other office-type jobs. For a couple of years there, I felt defective and stupid.

School or professional boredom bleeds into every area of your life. You start getting an "Is this all there is?" feeling. You're longing for something. This is when we usually turn to a delicious dysfunctional pattern with food, shopping, drinking, working out too much, or clinging to a really jacked-up relationship. Then you feel, "Okay, now *there's* a little somethin' somethin'. I'm still alive. I feel a charge. I can play around with all this other junk that has nothing to do with my actual heart and soul, but at least I'm entertained. Sah-weeeet."

But if you have to rely on outside stuff to feel alive and there's no energy in your work or school efforts, then you might not be doing what you want. Do not settle for the "Is all there is?" life plan. C'mon! Remember, you are here once in this life, with these gifts and values and callings. So why are you trying to get your life force from shopping too much and dating someone who makes you feel crappy? It won't work. And you know it.

As with resistance, it can be hard for you to spot the boredom thing in yourself. You don't want to admit that your life feels pointless, so you just focus on all of the distracting, stupid stuff. Again, the peeps closest to you may be able to point out this pattern. It'll bug you when your parents notice you're focused more on clothes than college essays, your friends call you out on having only gum for dinner, or your significant other mentions that you're drinking too much. And I know you're underage and maybe it's not cool for me to say that in a book for high school kids, but let's get real. During high school and college, I saw a lot a lot of guys, and a good number of gals, start drinking way too much for a lot of reasons. Similarly, I saw a lot of young women, myself included, not eat enough and work out too much. Some of this behavior has to do with not letting go of past pain, and some of it is due to current boredom or future anxiety. Whatever the case may be, none of these addictive patterns need to be a life sentence. See them for the symptoms they are and get some real help. You can bust out of it, and you'll be all the wiser and stronger for having gone through it.

A big contributing factor to all of these dysfunctional and addictive patterns that don't serve us is that you just don't know what you want. You've lost touch with your precious heart. You don't think you can consider what would really make your spirit soar. Who deserves to live out their dreams? Um, *you*! So if you feel bored out of your mind thinking about college or working on applications for certain schools, then maybe you are barking up the wrong tree. That doesn't mean you shouldn't be applying to college. But you should get honest about where you want to go, what you want to study, where you want to live, when you want to go, and whom you want to grow into while you're there. Let yourself think about it. Questioning is really healthy. What do you want?

It might feel as though the answer isn't coming fast enough. This is where space and quiet become very important. When your head and body are all crammed up with noise and busyness, you don't have any room for your genuine longings. Take some time. Sit. Get quiet. Walk around and ask yourself, what does the dog, the moon, the stop sign have to say about what I want? It sounds ridiculous, but if you keep putting the question out there and leave some space, the answers will come to you. You'll hear your Self answer back. You will feel what you want. It's in you. Deep down. Shhh. Listen.

Haste: It Really Does Make Waste

How do you handle something when you really don't want to do it? You do it quickly. It's the BAND-AID approach: rip it off, and it's over. Acting quickly is an avoidance technique so we can move on to the next seemingly more desirable activity. Crank out that Spanish homework; head off to basketball. Break it off with that girl via text; ask out the cute new one. Just get it done and go.

But the hasty approach to life is actually an obstacle to living your life. If you aren't aware of what you're doing and if you aren't deliberate in your actions, you aren't actually living here right now. You're jumping ahead. Who knows where you are. But you aren't in your life; you aren't in your body at this moment.

I see (and do) this all the time in yoga: when things get hard, we all move a lot faster. It's like drive-by yoga. Just hit that pose for an instant and get to the next and next and next until it's over and I can rest on my back and then jump up and run to the next thing and next and next. But the problem is, you aren't learning how to do any of the poses. They never get any easier, you never notice your patterns, and you don't move forward physically or mentally with the practice.

It's the same thing when you rush that Spanish homework to get to basketball. You end up needing to relearn the material for the next test or next semester because you didn't get it the first time around. Same thing with the breakup. You don't have a real conversation to end it initially and probably have to spend much more time later having a gross, hostile conversation because feelings got hurt. Or you both just waste time in your heads having a talk that should've happened. Ultimately, you don't get anywhere faster by rushing through stuff. On a bigger scale, this goes to the karmic idea of life lessons, which I discuss in more detail at the end of this chapter: if you rush through tricky situations unconsciously, then you don't learn the lessons and ultimately repeat them in some other scenario. Bummer.

Notice any hastiness with your college applications? Oh, say racing through SAT prep, cranking out halfhearted essays, randomly picking schools just to be done with the list? Parents tend to notice this stuff all the time, and we roll our eyes at them for it. "Why don't you slow down and pick up your room? Did you finish your SAT work? You're already done with your essays?" You've heard it. But you probably also see this in yourself. You can feel when you're rushing through something, avoiding doing it for real. You let yourself get distracted and waste your energy on things that don't really matter to you. Be honest with yourself about why you don't want to do the real task at hand and how you can go about slowing down.

We always want to be ahead of where we are. A big part of mindful living is to respect that there's a timeline to everything and, for the most part, we aren't in charge of it. You wish you could write faster. You wish you could get over your ex sooner. You wish you could learn the SAT words immediately. You want to be done with that part and move on to the next. But this is your life right now. You create a lot of stress and dissatisfaction for yourself by speeding to the next bit. Your life right now is learning the SAT words and thinking through essays. That's cool. It's this chapter. And when it's time to move on, you will. Step back and watch how nature moves. It's on its pace. Things fly and flow and rise and fall as they are supposed to. Try to be where you are with each phase of this process and accept that you're there. Soak up all there is to know, and you'll be in the next moment before you know it. In fact, you're there already. Next moment. And another and another.

When You're Stuck: Let It Go

My best friend in high school, Missy, was one of the first of us to leave for college. She was going to University of Wisconsin—Madison, and it started on the early side. We were having a great summer, working and hanging out. August was full of pool parties, making collages to take to school, packing up boxes, and a bit of dread. We wanted to go, but we weren't quite ready. Missy went into superavoidance mode. She got stuck and just would not pack for school, even though she was leaving soon. I remember her mom asking me if I could trick her into going to buy shampoo and toothpaste to at least get her toiletries packed up. But, hey, we understood Missy's pain because we all did the same thing two weeks later. We weren't ready to say good-bye.

The stuck thing is a big one. You get so comfortable with where you are that you avoid letting it end, even when it has to. So many of us got stuck during the application phase. It's similar to resistance in that you avoid what you need to do to move forward, like writing essays, but it's a bit more of full-blown denial or sadness. You won't do it. You won't open the college information, and the mail piles up. You won't talk with your parents about where you want to go on your school visits. You don't make appointments with your guidance counselor. You're like a mule with your hooves pushing into the ground: *I'm not doing this!*

We get stuck when something is ending and we don't feel ready to let it go. Maybe it's a natural ending, like high school being over. Maybe it's an ending that requires some thought on your part, like your high school relationship being over. Maybe it's a bigger ending, like your childhood being over. Big stuff. Heavy. It deserves respect and attention.

You need good endings to make space for great beginnings. Until you get closure, you drift around and miss the next big opportunity in life. You don't move forward in life as a whole until you learn the lessons and pass the tests of your current grade. You can't start college until you pack your toiletries. Our friends and families will see this stuckness in us. Just as I had to drive Missy to the Giant Pharmacy to buy Crest, your mom may point out that it's time to make a list of schools for applications, and your girlfriend may break up with you knowing it's for the best. Don't hate the messenger. They are trying to help you.

As a first step to loosening the stuckness, it can help to acknowledge the endings and beginnings you see around you all the time. Each time you exhale, you empty out completely, making space for the new inhale. Notice the change of seasons and recognize that you, too, cycle through them. People have quiet, still, reflective times like winter, and we burst open with possibilities like spring. We slow down and get a little lazy like summer. We reap what we've sown like fall.

The transition from high school to college is an epic ending on many fronts. Do not brush it off. Give special attention to the different endings you face to make space for the new. Let your teachers and coaches help you organize ceremonies for your clubs and teams; give people a chance to express their feelings around saying good-bye. You'll have graduation and prom and such, but make special time with your close friends to acknowledge that you're leaving each other. Let yourselves be sad and reflective; it only shows how wonderful your time together has been. Your friendships will enter a different and still lovely season when you call each other at college and help each other out. Be mindful of whether your high school relationship should continue. Have respect for that significant other and really think about what is best for the two of you. Let yourself have personal letting go ceremonies, again with journaling, being outside, dancing, singing, running, or whatever it is you love to do. Just infusing regular acts with intention will make them spiritual and healing.

The more you can let go of what is naturally leaving, the more space you will create for the new that is naturally coming.

Got It! Wait, Do I?

I felt pretty good going into my first day of teaching third grade at Lockwood Year Round School in Oakland, California. I'd been teaching hip-hop dance in the Cambridge schools for three years. During the summers, I'd led a camp for kids in the housing projects near school and taught literature and dance through Summerbridge. My summer teaching at the Teach For America institute in Houston had been fine. I knew enough to know that I didn't know everything, but I felt confident.

Teach For America assigned me an older mentor, a Teach For America teacher who had continued to teach in Oakland for a few years. He was a great guy, and we became good friends quickly, especially as my fabulous roommate developed a whopper of a crush on him. (And him on her, though he was loathe to admit it!) He told me that as long as none of my students bled from the head on the first day, then I should consider it as success. Ha ha. As if my standards were so low. I was going to set up my classroom management systems, get them writing in their journals, and be strict but kind. I was ready.

On my first day, I welcomed 35 third graders into my room. That's a lot of third graders. Twenty-three of them were boys. The women's study major in me quickly changed my tune on nurture trumping nature as I watched the girls dutifully open their new journals to write while the boys threw pencils in a solid attempt to take someone's eye out. The first question posed of me that day was, "How old are you? Like 16?" Thank you, Derrick. Guess that my suit didn't do the trick.

Somehow I got them halfway listening, and after journal time, we set about practicing walking in line. I was being proactive on the classroom management front, and managing 35 eight-year-olds in a line takes a good bit of management. As we made our way through the hall at 10:45 AM, I felt like a champ. There had been some journal writing. Now all 35 were sort of quietly walking in line. Okay, I've got this. This year is going to be great! And then, "Ms. Malachuk!" I turned to see that Antwaney had chosen this moment to play with her loose teeth and successfully ripped the front two out a bit earlier than they wanted to leave her mouth. Blood was shooting out of her face in every direction. The first day would not be a success.

After the head bleed of day one at Lockwood, things actually got much worse. I had a really hard time getting that class under control. Those boys put me through the ringer. For the first two weeks, my principal actually assigned one of our school security guard types to hang out in my room. Fortunately, I cared more about becoming a good teacher for those kids than about being an immediate wunderkind success. My ego took a backseat while I asked for help from every party imaginable on how to manage my classroom. I will be forever grateful to Ms. Stovall and Ms. DeWitt for dropping some serious wisdom my way. Though it never got easy, not for one second, my kids and I became a good team. And I figured out how to manage a classroom quite well. I ended up being a resource for teachers on how to set up systems and keep a classroom humming along. I learned a ton that year that I hadn't known I needed to learn.

My point is that just when you think you've got life figured out, you might want to check again. It's cool though. In some ways, you've got it going on, but in some ways, you need a helping hand.

We all have moments of false peaks, when we think we've reached the top only to look and see we're nowhere near it. It's resting at that false peak and deciding you know everything that is your obstacle to moving forward.

I'll confess to thinking I knew quite a bit during senior year of high school. Adults seemed increasingly idiotic. The guidance counselor was worthless. I brushed off a lot of my parents' suggestions on how to choose schools. My brothers didn't understand the pressure, never mind that they'd been through it recently. No one could help me. I don't think I was alone in developing a bit of a 'tude. We're so stressed about our stuff that we don't want to listen to anyone. I've got it. Just leave me alone!

In this year of applying and graduating and moving on, look for wisdom everywhere. Seek out advice. Take in unsolicited advice. Open yourself up to what people have to say. A passing bit could inspire a thought for essays. An unlikely source may suggest just the right school for you. The breathing exercises in this book could help you chill out and make it through the process. Life would be totally boring if you knew all the answers at the start. Life's a practice, not a show. You're growing as you go, even now when you think you've got the answers. Humility and self-awareness are the hallmarks of maturity. Cultivate your curiosity and soak up the lessons. You're not supposed to get it all right now, or ever. Just keep seeking.

Keep in Mind You're Part of a Bigger Picture

There are times when all applicants want to pull out their hair and scream, "For the love of God, can I please get through these applications?" Perhaps the most powerful step you can take as an applicant is to take that plea literally.

Yoga alert! Yoga alert! Things are about to get touchy-feely and a bit spiritual here, so feel free to skip it. Or give it a read and see if there's something you can take away.

A great way to deal with immediate stress or challenges in your life is to step back and recognize that this moment is only one part of your big and awesome journey. Remember the hero's journey from chapter 3 on essays? When things get rough, you're in lesson-learning mode. As you focus on your efforts and let go of the results, know that you have resources of strength, resilience, and hope far beyond anything your brain can imagine.

I'm talking about tapping into that bigger force at play in your life and the universe: the uber-force of goodness, peace, joy, contentment, and bliss. Yoga philosophy offers us the idea that a massively loving and peaceful force is within each of us; it's that Self idea we've been talking about. As you reveal your Self and nurture the love and light within you, you can see and support the love and light in everyone else, as well. Further, by connecting with your own peace and love, you connect with the ultimate source of this love and grace, which is beyond all of us. Explaining that force is beyond the scope of this book—or even my brain. I'm just one small person sitting at her laptop, grateful that my current job is putting words on a page; I'm not in the business of figuring out the meaning of life.

That said, speaking from my heart to yours, we all know that feeling of connecting to this limitless force of contentment and grace. Maybe even if just for a moment, we've all felt peacefully insignificant in the massive circle of life, and we've all felt infinitely loving as we've walked through the world. Maybe? A little? It finds us in different places at different times, whether we're looking or not. It's *awesome* in the true sense of the word, inspiring awe. Some people like to think about God, Allah, or the universe, and others don't want to give it any kind of name at all. My point is that connecting to that force of strength and grace that is inside you can be not only sanity saving but also inspiring during a time of massive stress and transition, like when applying to college. So do your work, offer up your results, and have faith that everything's going to work out for you.

Again, I hear you on all of this, "What does that mean? Work out for me? I've got a bunch of stress in my life, and cultivating faith as a strategy seems a little loosey-goosey." But here's the deal—and hang in there, because even if you aren't totally down with the yoga thing, this information can help you—yoga teaches us that we have two choices in each moment: fear or faith. Our human self pushes fear: you cling to the known to protect yourself. Fear tells you to hide, compete, and control, and you tend to play life small. In contrast, your higher Self inspires faith: it enables you to leap into the unknown to celebrate your spirit. Faith helps you to expand, trust, give, and play life big. Right now, as you're embarking on going to college and becoming an independent adult, you want to play it big. The world wants you to play it big.

When you're applying to schools or during any time of transition, the fear voice loves to attach to specific dreams of our futures. How cozy and controlling to daydream exactly where you'll get into college and how it will be when you find out and whom you'll tell and what they'll say and how you'll feel. You can play the scene out over and over again in your mind. But this type of obsessing is preventing you from actually experiencing your life right now, and it's also preventing you from living your biggest version of yourself. Although anticipation is delicious, daydreaming is actually pretty limiting. You're stuck in your mind with this very particular result. Even if it's a so-called "good" result, you're still keeping yourself in a small space by having a defined outcome. Maybe there's a more beautiful and brilliant possibility waiting for you, something even sweeter than your brain can imagine. Faith is about letting go of specific desires and staying open to endless possibilities.

Okay, but what happens when you stay in the moment, keep an open mind about your possibilities, and then get rejected by Vanderbilt? I'm not gonna lie; it's a bummer. But having faith means trusting that you can get through anything, and your story sure doesn't end with your acceptance or rejection from college. Your story never ends; you are constantly working to open yourself up and learn more. It's a continual process of revealing your Self. That's the real game here. Not getting into Pomona. Here's where a deeper understanding of karma can be helpful in developing faith—time for a karma break-it-down.

The Sanskrit word *karma* is translated as "action" or "deed." Every action is the effect of a previous action and the cause of a future action; thus, every action is karma. *What does karma have to do with my getting into college?* Hang with me here. What this means is that basically, everything you do comes from something you've done before, and it creates what you do next. In Western culture, we tend to think of karma in a superficial sense—in terms of *payback*: for example, when you do something, it comes back at you. It could be related events—like if you dump someone, then you get dumped. (Think Justin Timberlake's "What Goes Around Comes Around.") Or it could be seemingly unrelated events—like if you get snippy with your mom on the phone and then you trip on the sidewalk. In some ways, both of those examples are right on, yet they only scratch the surface of what's up with karma.

The real karmic lessons are going on in your mind. That's where true cause and effect takes place, since your thoughts determine your actions and how you view your world. As a white chick who grew up in suburban Maryland, I am not the world's foremost authority on karma, so let's turn to Eknath Easwaran, an Indian scholar who has taught in the West: he (2007, 34) explains that "karma is sometimes considered punitive, a matter of getting one's just desserts [sic]." (Here is where Justin Timberlake is right on: "Girl, you cheat on me; someone cheats on you!") But Easwaran goes on to say that "it is much more illuminating to consider karma an educative force." These karmic lessons are helping people act in accordance with the flow of humanity; karma helps us "not to pursue selfish interests at the expense of others, but to contribute to life and consider the welfare of the whole." Karma helps you reveal your highest Self. You learn some lessons, while not quite getting others, with the ultimate goal of revealing your Self here on earth, acting from a place of compassion and love as opposed to competition and fear. Easwaran says, "In this sense life is like a school; one can learn, one can graduate, one can skip a grade or stay behind." So here on earth, you learn life lessons and do your best.

This goes back to the idea that being "successful" in life is not about *what* you do but *how* you do it. Are you staying present to recognize these lessons? Are you releasing specific outcomes and instead looking at the bigger picture? Are you shedding your fearful human behavior to operate from your loving, faith-filled Self? Can you move from a place of love instead of fear in your actions day in and day out? It's the old "Love thy neighbor as thyself" credo. Plus, there's a ripple effect, and what you put out comes back. Your actions go on and on and on in small and big ways. Your thoughts and behavior create your immediate world but also the state of humanity. Karma helps you take responsibility for your life and, really, for all of our lives. Karma also helps you keep the faith that you're working on something a bit bigger than what you're facing in this moment.

So when things get tough, rather than being scared, stressed, and fearful, you can get curious and take action. You can look at your life more symbolically, scouring your actions and thoughts for opportunities to learn lessons, shake up your patterns, and view your life in an open, hopeful, and faith-filled way. Of course, sometimes it can take a while to see or understand the lesson. It's like math class, when you keep getting one type of problem wrong until you hear it explained in a different way. At business school, we had an economics professor who didn't understand this basic element of teaching. He would explain a concept, and we'd be confused and ask questions. He'd say the same thing but use a green pen instead of a black one on the white board. Look, dude, it's not the pen color that's blocking my understanding here! I need to see a different example!

In this sense, we are all each other's teachers, giving each other situations so we can see things in a new way and learn lessons. In fact, some of your best teachers can be the people who drive you crazy. If you have a controlling boyfriend, recognize that he's helping you learn the costs of not speaking your truth and telling him to get lost. When you're in a long line at the grocery store, the painfully slow checker is helping you cultivate patience. Because actually you are giving these teachers the power to bring you lessons. That part of you that is scared to speak your truth is encouraging that boyfriend to be controlling. That part of you that is impatient is viewing the grocery checker as slow.

Whether the situation is big or small, you are in charge of finding lessons and growing in your thoughts and behavior. This notion can help you lose the victim mentality when ruminating over tough situations or old, painful stories about your life. Instead of blaming others, you can see how you're contributing to situa-

tions, perhaps even drawing these people and events to you to learn
your lessons. So when you step back and see limiting, frustrating, negative patterns in your life, recognize that you yourself are
bringing about these lessons to help you move forward. I've heard
it said that life whispers first, then when you don't pick up the
lessons, life will shout. So pay attention and try to move forward
before the shouting begins.

That said, horrific things may have happened to you, and it
may seem unfathomable to you that you would bring those situations on yourself. I've heard a few karmic takes on this type of
thing—that you've been caught up in someone else's karma or that
your higher Self knows it needs your human self to go through
some terrible earthly situations to be truly revealed. Regardless,
it is a faith-filled response to know that you can learn from each
and every situation and move forward to become a bigger, more
open, loving you. This is when the Aha! moments start flowing. You start to see clearly that you're getting back what you're
putting out on a physical and energetic level. Have patience with
yourself, though. It can take a while to move forward in our life
lessons. Oprah often quotes Maya Angelou as saying, "When you
know better, you do better." All of this karma talk can help you
have some faith in yourself. You are doing your best, and in each
moment, you are exactly where you need to be, facing the lessons
you want to learn.

Right now in this moment and all the ones to follow, you can
decide how this college application process goes for you. It's not
about whether you get into the supposed college of your choice or

not. It's about how you approach it, full of fear or full of faith. You have the choice to look to your higher Self and your higher source for grace during the difficult times and practice gratitude for the lessons you're learning along the way. You, not some admissions committee, are in charge of your life. Your inner voice, your Self, can guide you through this.

You may face grades, SATs, and essays now, but obstacles will continue to surface throughout your life. Don't see that as a bummer. These obstacles and stresses are teachable moments that illuminate valuable lessons when you're losing your way. If you stay aware and present, you will work your way through them and be a better version of you for it. Also, as you see with most of them, the way out is just being present, getting still, and letting answers come to you. Although this requires knowing yourself and taking responsibility for your own life, remember that you are not floating out in the seas by yourself. People around you love you and are poised and ready to help you out. Sometimes, that's a tough love of pointing out when things don't seem right; sometimes, it's lending a hand to get you back on track. Know that you're part of a web of connection and all you need to do is reach out.

Moreover, there's your infinite source of grace and love that's always out there—and in you. That massive source of peace, joy, and contentment abides in each of us. Whenever you want, you can tap into the faith of knowing that you're exactly where you need to be and you have the inner resources to deal with anything. Your highest, most magnificent Self is waiting to be revealed more and more with your next steps, and you know just what to do.

Learn to love and take care of yourself, and remember that you are never alone.

✦ ✦ ✦

Keeping the faith and recognizing that this is just one moment of your life truly become the name of the game as we head into our next chapter on waiting and decisions.

CHAPTER 6

❖

The Waiting Game — and Then Decision Time

You Own Your Life, so Live It *Now*

You've sent in your applications! Yee haw! Over the next couple of months, a million people will say this to you: "Now all you have to do is wait." They are well intentioned, hoping to comfort you by saying there's nothing more you can do. It's out of your hands. You can rest and wait. Fine. Except waiting is a total nightmare. Even if you aren't taking any more direct action to communicate with schools, your mind is going nutso. The waiting period is a festival of fantasies about whether you'll get in or not and what that will feel like. Your body is going to school, going to track practice, doing homework, playing piano, painting pictures, hanging out with friends, but your mind is four months, six months, a year in the future imagining life at your dream school—or, yikes, not.

Perhaps the only thing worse than waiting is actually hearing from schools. I'll never forget returning home from spring break to find the letters waiting for me. (Letters, I know, how old-school.) My respectful parents let me go into the house by myself so I could have a moment alone. I felt sick as I opened the door. A week's worth of mail was lying on the floor of our front hall. I dropped onto my knees and sorted through, looking for large packets. I didn't see any. Instead I found thin letters from Duke, Brown, Stanford, and Tufts and slightly thicker letter-size envelopes from Bowdoin and Northwestern. I tore them open. Duke—rejected. Brown—rejected. Stanford—rejected. Tufts—wait-listed. Bowdoin—accepted. Northwestern—accepted.

Rejection. So much rejection. Shamefully, I'll admit to not one moment of gratitude for the acceptances to Bowdoin and Northwestern. Instead, I burst into hysterical tears, telling my parents I didn't get in anywhere, meaning not Duke. I ran to my car and drove to my boyfriend's house; he was still a junior and, thus, above the college fray. When his mom saw me weeping in the kitchen, he said, "Kate's crying because she didn't get into Duke, so she has to go to Northwestern." Her response, "Northwestern's a better school than Duke." A moment of perspective? Sadly, no. My only thought was that maybe others shared her opinion and wouldn't see me as the failure I was. Totally concerned with others, opinions. Ego at the helm!

Waiting, rejection, decisions... it's all so gross. But instead of putting yourself at the mercy of schools, you can stop the madness. This is a chapter about how to take back the power, how to make this period of waiting a great time for you, how to see the acceptances and rejections as information and not judgments, and how to make decisions about your future based on who you are and what you want. Remember, you own your life.

You Can Either Wait For the Future or Enjoy Your Life *Now*

Here's the deal. This period of waiting is really no different from any other time in your life. In fact, if you let your chattering mind run the show, all of life can feel like waiting because you're always thinking towards the future. Waiting to get through physics class so you can go to lunch. Waiting to get taller so girls will dig you. Waiting for that guy to ask you to prom. Waiting to graduate high school so you can lose the curfew. Waiting to get through freshman year of college so you can move out of the dorms. Waiting to visit your long-distance girlfriend or boyfriend. Waiting to get done with pre-med requirements. Waiting to find out what job you get after college. Waiting to finish two years of investment banking. Waiting to graduate from law school. Waiting to make partner at the firm. Waiting to meet the right life partner. Waiting for the right time to start a family. Waiting to sell your house and retire.

You get the point. We do a lot of waiting. Each minute or chapter of life can feel like something you need to get through to move on to the next good part. But really, the key to happiness and fulfillment is to stop waiting and start living right now.

So here's a subversive idea. Try using this ultimate waiting period, between applying to and hearing from colleges, to practice being super present. Make this time a boot camp for living in the moment. Rather than pitching your mind ahead to graduation and college, get incredibly interested in what you are doing right now.

A first step towards being in the moment is a very low maintenance meditation practice. This may sound boring (but it feels great!) or difficult (but it's just breathing!). Even if you're skeptical, you might want to give it a go because it can be a game changer in your life. Meditation is simply the practice of using your mind to notice your mind. Remember chapters 1 and 2? We did a few of these simple exercises then: just find a quiet place, take a comfortable position (sitting or lying down), and choose a focus point for your mind like your breath. Then just follow your breath, coming in and going out. Your mind is going to wander off of the breath. When you notice your mind has wandered (like every two seconds!), bring it back to the breath. Over and over again.

The noticing is what's important when you do the practice of meditation. You are cultivating a part of you that's watching, a piece that can help you take a step back from your thoughts. In fact, you see that you are more than your thoughts. Perhaps you can choose what to do with thoughts. Rather than being dragged into the past and future, you can choose to be *here, now.* If there's choice in what thoughts you follow, then there's also choice in how you act based on those thoughts. Often, we just unconsciously think and react. With meditation, you start to see space between you and your thoughts, between you and your actions. You choose how to be in this world. In fact, you are creating your world with the thoughts and actions you select. Empowering, no?

Also, in meditation, you can see just how rapidly your mind dances around. As you watch your thoughts (sometimes with horror), you can take solace in their impermanence. Even if you do get tripped up and follow your thoughts down the rabbit holes of depression, anxiety, and fear, no emotional state is permanent. We talked about this earlier. Remember, just as your thoughts change and change, so do your emotions.

You know how when you first have a crush on someone and it's unclear how the other party feels? She flirts with you during math, and you're giddy throughout class. You see her flirting with someone else in the hall, and you're moping throughout English. She sits next to you at lunch, and you're on top of the world again. What a difference 30 minutes makes! But you're letting yourself get tossed about based on external circumstances, whether or not she pays attention to you. The same thing happens in everyone's lives, in every situation. Rejected from Brandeis today—ack! Accepted by Purdue tomorrow—whew! Lose your football game today—ack! Throw the winning touchdown pass tomorrow—whew! Nothing is permanent. Things always change. Meditation helps you rest with the impermanence of thoughts and emotions so you can practice being cool with the impermanence of life.

I know it's a little scary to think of nothing being permanent. But again, this idea will set you free. Embracing impermanence can help you chill. Thoughts will come and go, things will come and go, people will come and go. As we discussed, if you try to cling to the past or project to the future, you're setting yourself up for suffering. So this waiting period is a fantastic time in your life for becoming skilled at nonattachment, precisely because this time is so ripe for attaching to fantasies of your future. Remember, if you can let go of specific ideas of what should happen to you, you are setting yourself up for bigger and better things than you can even imagine. Letting go leaves space for the new to come in. If you're so fixated on your old boyfriend, you won't meet someone new. If you're so obsessed with going to Berkeley, you'll miss the chance to learn that Occidental is a great fit for you. Once you clean out the clutter of attachments in your mind and focus on just being yourself, you will be amazed at the people and opportunities that flow right into your world.

A quick note on how tough this all is. Notice that the language I use around being present and nonattachment is *practice* or *becoming skilled*. That's because being present and releasing attachments are no easy tasks. They are probably the hardest things for our human minds to do. Staying present and letting go are lifelong tasks, and times like waiting to hear from colleges are great opportunities to skip a grade level in the school of life and get clear that all you truly need is already within you.

Finally, as mentioned, this so-called waiting time is a great opportunity to start being your own guru around balance in your life. When you're in the fall of senior year and thick in application mode, your life is bound to be imbalanced, skewing towards all work and very little play. So be it. Those times happen. Key is to stay aware of what you're doing, recognize that you're imbalanced, and try to take care of yourself mentally and physically.

But second semester of senior year, you'll have a little more time on your hands. Oh yeah. You can look at how you're actually spending your moments. Meditation can help with this, too. There's a great book on meditation by Sakyong Mipham, a Tibetan Buddhist scholar, called *Turning the Mind into an Ally*. I know, I know, a Tibetan Buddhist scholar... he can't understand your world. Actually, he grew up in Boulder, Colorado, because his father was there bringing Buddhism to America. He plays golf, runs marathons, and wears those long maroon monk robes with Ray-Bans, which is a surprisingly good look. A Western guy with an Eastern perspective, he (2004, 216) writes, "Beginning meditation practice is an excellent opportunity to contemplate how we spend our time. How much of what we do is important and truly necessary?... What drains us; what nourishes us?"

Ooh, looking at what drains us and what nourishes us. Love that. He's talking about following your energy and getting curious about what brings you bliss. It's tempting to waste second semester of senior year doing nothing. Instead, though, you could use it to play around with new stuff or do a deep dive into things you already love. It's valuable time to see what makes your Self sing out. Take that elective in ceramics, try out for the musical, join a band, or play a club sport. As I write this, I'm remembering that my guy friends spent a lot of time watching MTV, and that's important, too. Maybe your heart is longing for you to be more outgoing and focus on your friendships. Check out that Wheel of Life from chapter 4 and see where you're putting your energy. Maybe you can spread it around. See what's exciting and interesting to you. Instead of *fantasizing* about what you'll do or who you'll be in college, you could try *doing* those things and *being* that person right now. What's the point of waiting? There's no better time than the present.

Decisions, Decisions

Before you know it, decisions will be upon you — *your* decisions about what to do next in your life. Oh, I'm sorry, did you think someone else would be doing the deciding about your life... say, the admissions committees? Yes, well, they are lovely people doing difficult work, but they aren't in charge of your life. *You* are.

Of course, whom are we kidding? The admissions committee is going to toss a big decision in your face. In the end, they will accept you or reject you. They may string you along with a deferral or a wait-list, but in the end, it'll be yes or no. Simple as that. This is a glorious opportunity to practice not taking their decision as a judgment about you — a skill you're going to need big-time in your life, if you want to work on revealing your Self instead of being who you think others want you to be.

The Admissions Committee's Decision
Isn't a Judgment about You Personally

Before we get too excited about disregarding the admissions committee's opinions, let's give them some credit for being good at their job. Acceptances and rejections, in the college world, are about a lot of factors. The admissions committees are building a class. They have a billion more qualified applicants than spaces, plus they have to figure out how to create a balanced group of first years. I saw the genius behind how they create a class when I got to business school at Stanford. Because our class was so small (about 350 people), you could see all of the different talents, interests, and backgrounds we each had that made a delicious stew of a class. My classes at Harvard and Northwestern were larger, so the diversity was less obvious, but the same idea was at play. As we discussed in chapter 1, the diversity of college makes it one of the richest experiences of your life. Schools want to provide you with the opportunity to learn from your classmates and teach them, as well. The admissions committees know that they can't take everyone who would be great in the stew, but it's not easy for them to leave out fabulous you. Know that people labored over these decisions and did not take them lightly.

Which brings us to the next truth about admissions committees: they care about you. Admissions committees are made up of regular people with hearts and emotions who want you to develop into a happy, healthy college student. For real. They are cool and thoughtful and on your side. They know who is going to be a fit for the school. Even if we as applicants have done all of our homework and convinced ourselves that we belong at Williams, the admissions committee there may know better. I know this down to the bottom of my heart from my time as director of admissions at Teach For America. It was extremely painful to reject people who were sure they should be doing Teach For America when we could see that it wasn't the right fit for them professionally at that time. You come to know applicants extremely well through essays, interviews, and recommendations—and you care about them. I recently ran into a friend from high school who told me that when her little brother was a senior at Georgetown, he got a rejection letter from Teach For America signed by me. I felt awful hearing this, even years after the fact, but if he wasn't a good fit, then he wasn't a good fit. The admissions committees are doing what they think is best when they don't accept you. It's a little tough love, but remember, they have your interests at heart.

Finally, you shouldn't take rejection as a judgment because it's just not a judgment. It's many things coming together and sometimes a mystery. I have seen so many friends and applicants get into some schools and not others, and sometimes it makes no sense. They were just as qualified and seemingly the right fit at the schools where they were rejected, but it just wasn't meant to be. A rejection from a college simply means that for some reason, you are not supposed to be going to that school at this time. Who knows why? So just leave it at that. Life is actually a big mystery when lived well. In time, some of these mysterious events may make perfect sense, and others not so much. In the immortal words of the Beatles, "Let it be."

If You Don't Get What You Think You Want, Don't Get Stuck

Let it be and then move on. Being rejected from your dream school is a beautiful moment to relax into the ebb and flow of life, consider other options, and get more real about your dreams. Parker Palmer (1999, 54), an inspiring writer and leader in higher education, writes that "each time a door closes, the rest of the world opens up. All we need to do is stop pounding on the door that just closed, turn around—which puts the door behind us—and welcome the largeness of life that now lies open to our souls. The door that closed kept us from entering a room, but what now lies before us is the rest of reality." We miss so many opportunities and lessons because we keep banging on that closed door. Once we turn around and move forward as ourselves, it is amazing what our Self has in store for us. Really, the best things in life are those that take us by surprise, that appear simply because we are living our truth.

Take rejections and acceptances as information. That's all they are. We infuse them with pain and joy. Really, though, they are just information. This school is not an option, but that one is. From there, this process is about *you* making decisions on how to move forward. Rejections and acceptances are going to happen over and over again throughout your life with schools, romantic relationships, friendships, talent shows, book clubs, sports teams, fraternities, sororities, jobs ... they happen all the time. Right now is a chance to practice detaching from the rollercoaster of emotions to think about what *you* really want. You don't have to be defeated by rejections; you can reconsider what was important to you about what you didn't get and then move on with a clearer picture of what you want and need in a person, school, job, etc. Similarly, you don't have to blindly take acceptances; you can think about what is appealing and what doesn't feel right about the person, school, or job and then make a choice. Either way, *you* are in charge of the steps you take in your life.

Life Can Take You Places You Didn't Even Know You Wanted to Go

So many people I know and have worked with have taken steps around college and life in general that seem out of the ordinary and have been all the better for it. In fact, it's usually these different moves that other people want to hear about, whether during job interviews or when hanging out at parties, because these unusual twists and turns mark a time when you answered something deep within you. These times when we answer a calling to do something a little different reveal our gifts and values, and they are often the richest times in our lives. Of course, some people get into their dream schools and go and are all done. Nothing wrong with that! Plus, there are so many amazing things to do during college, including study-abroad opportunities, that even if your path unfolds traditionally, so to speak, you'll be up to your ears in options to explore different paths. But let's look at a bunch of different stories just to bust open the mythical path of "get accepted to favorite school and go."

Sometimes "Not Your First Choice" Can Be Your Best Choice

The most common scenario is that you get into a handful of schools, maybe your reaches and maybe not, and you start that fall. Most people I know who went off to "not their dream school" ended up being really happy — because college is wonderful. But some people had specific reasons why they were grateful not to get into their reach schools in the end. One friend who was rejected by Yale said that going to Oberlin let him see that there were other options than "New York City — prep school — Harvard or Yale"; getting outside of the Ivy League box let him think more expansively about his life options. Great point.

Similarly, others ended up trying a new part of the country. "I didn't think I'd end up going to University of Texas — Austin, but then it was the best place I got in, and I ended up loving Texas!" And the romantics who met their wife or husband at college are, of course, grateful that they ended up at that school to meet their beloved.

One interesting scenario is when you have a secret doubt that your dream school isn't your dream. One super-cool applicant really wanted to go to a fancy, big-name East Coast school. She had an interesting mix going on: she was raised in a very sheltered religious community but had a ripping sense of humor and was interested in journalism and politics. She was also the best writer I've seen in all my years of reading any essays. Phenomenal. She was rejected from the fancy East Coast school but accepted at many others, including Northwestern. I was prepared to hear a very sad girl because of that one rejection.

Instead, she had done some thinking and said that honestly she wasn't sure about the big East Coast school deep in her heart. She was from the East Coast and eager to see someplace with a different atmosphere and mentality than that of her youth. Again, sometimes admissions committees are smarter than we are. Something wasn't quite right between the East Coast school and her. You could never tell on paper, but it was just off. She felt as though she'd dodged a bullet and happily ventured off to Northwestern.

On that note, even if you get into your super-dream-reach school, pause and consider. Make sure you are going because *you* want to go there, not because someone else wants you to or you think you have to. Remember that getting in doesn't mean anything other than that. *You* decide if it's the right place for you.

Time Off before College Can Be a Blessing in Disguise

But let's look at some stories that veer off the beaten path, so to speak. One friend was accepted by a fancy-pants Ivy League school out of high school ... but for the following year. Say what? It wasn't a rejection, but they were asking her to take a gap year. She could have started school at one of the other awesome places she got in to, but she wanted to go there. So she took the gap. She worked but also spent months in Africa on a service-learning trip. She hadn't been to Africa before, and she fell in love with it. She had grown up going to preppy private schools in New England, but

Africa felt like home to her. Once at said fancy-pants school, she majored in anthropology and spent another semester and a summer in Africa doing senior thesis research. She has gone on to a fabulously successful career in public health and spends a ton of time in Africa. That time off was the gift of all gifts; it delivered her to her life's work.

Some folks take that gap year on purpose just to learn more about themselves. I have one friend who got into Wesleyan. Hooray. But he didn't go right out of the gate. Instead, he went to Paris for a year. When I asked him why, he said, "I wanted to get better at speaking French and learn to play the piano." Okay? While in Paris, he lived with a family, which was great, except that he was a big 18-year-old American boy, and they didn't eat between meals nor did they have snacks in the house. Ouch. He went to high school there, doing a postgraduate year of sorts, to improve his French. Like any nonnative speaker in school, he developed a love for math—all numbers, no words. It awoke a quantitative side in him, and he became interested in engineering. He returned home and decided to major in physics at Wesleyan, a strange move coming from his house of artistic humanities major types. He's now a writer, who went to business and journalism schools and can still play the piano and pull off some French—a true Renaissance man, thanks to a little detour before college.

My brother Mike is an example of someone taking a postgraduate year in school for athletic reasons. He didn't get the Division I basketball scholarship offer he so badly wanted out of high school. He had the option to go to University of Delaware and try to walk on, but he dreamed of a scholarship. So he spent a year at Fork Union Military Academy to get more exposure to Division I coaches and boost his academic record. His head coach, Coach Arritt, ended up being one of the big gurus of Mike's life. As difficult as it was to not go to college when his friends did and instead march around in a military uniform and share a bathroom with no stall doors (none, everything exposed, whoa), it was worth it to Mike to fulfill that dream and ultimately gain that valuable mentor. He headed off to University of Vermont on a scholarship the following year.

Or maybe you need to make some money, no matter whether or where you got accepted or rejected. I've seen many business school applicants who took time off before or during college to work, and they were all wiser for it. Some were exploring areas of interest, others were helping family businesses, others served in the military, and others were just trying to make a buck in whatever job they could get. The family business stories are always heartening, as people try to give back to their parents who have provided for them and perhaps train for taking over the biz in the future. Of course, the folks who serve in the military develop invaluable leadership and perspective. If you're going the more traditional job route, it can be difficult to find a position that's completely in line with your passions when you're just out of high school, but you will still gain a ton of character and wisdom from whatever work you do. When you're young and stuck waiting tables or doing administrative work, you learn a lot about yourself and your stamina (especially waiting tables—brutal!) and the way the world works.

With my stopping and starting of schools, I've temped a bit in my day. I've learned about the pharmaceutical industry and commercial real estate just from being the admin staff at various places for a bit. Sometimes the work can be interesting. Also, there's an important karmic life lesson to be learned. People in whatever office I ended up in for the day/week/month usually had no idea that I was starting Harvard or had just left Georgetown Law. While informative, it's a bummer to watch people be snotty to you because they assume you don't have a college degree. Working in lower-paying jobs makes it easy for you to do the karmic math on how you should treat people when you are higher in the ranks.

In general, working is always a great option, because no matter whether you love or hate the job, it gives you some financial resources, some purpose when you aren't sure where you are right now, and even some clues on what to pursue or leave behind. Knowing what you don't want is as important as knowing what you do want. That goes for jobs, schools, cities, relationships, etc. Some of the jobs I've hated most have been the best in terms of helping me follow my bliss.

What if You Don't Get In—Anywhere?

What about when you get rejected across the board? I had one MBA applicant who was phenomenal—he had everything schools were looking for, including a diverse background. His admissions essays were awesome. He got rejected everywhere. It made *no* sense. He's a very soulful and thoughtful guy, and we had a big heart-to-heart about the situation. He could have stayed in his private equity job and reapplied the next year, but he decided this rejection was an offer to let loose on the reins a bit. That said, he still wanted to reapply to schools. But he decided to pretend schools didn't exist and take a risk to do what he wanted with his professional life, which was international development.

During the application season, he had connected with an alum of one of the schools and helped him organize a fund-raiser for an international nonprofit. He went back to that alum, who offered him an unpaid internship for the summer doing work in South America. He took a risk and did that job, which led to a paid position doing international development. His bosses supported his reapplying to school, and now he's headed off to his dream school—but he has a much clearer sense of possibilities and real-world connections around the work he wants to do after graduation. Moreover, he's the happiest, most excited dude right now because he learned so much, traveled, and had a great time.

But I understand that getting rejected from all of your colleges and facing the reality of living at home with no game plan is different from having the fallback of staying at your six-figure private equity job. First, if you're rejected across the board, there's the reality of making some money. This goes back to the unglamorous but totally worthwhile job options that will help you get by and give you some control. Again, working always makes you feel better because a job gives some immediate purpose and structure to your days, and you can learn the deepest of lessons in the most mundane of pursuits.

Even if you are working full-time, you have a great opportunity to take some risks and explore outside interests before reapplying to colleges. During my dropout semester, my internship at the National Organization for Women was my chance to explore my interests in politics and feminism, interests that I followed by majoring in women's studies. Of course, that internship wasn't paid, so I was waiting tables, too. That said, I was living at home, and my parents weren't charging me rent. My tips from waiting tables went to social expenses (which were zippo because all of my friends were at college) and an Outward Bound trip. I was very fortunate. In general, though, it was nice to combine unpaid but stimulating work with paid grunt work.

If an internship isn't the right fit, you can explore interests at community college or night school classes; sometimes those are very affordable. Or maybe you want to find a way to develop passions without formal training, like taking up guitar or auditioning for community theater. You'll get to know yourself better and make better school selection choices the next time around. As mentioned, my second application process was very different after I'd done some soul-searching. I had a much better sense of what I wanted, where I would be a good fit, and how to express myself. Focus on getting to know yourself and doing research on schools so that reapplying will be a smoother process.

Or maybe you'll have the great fortune of time and resources to do a service project, whether you're rejected, just looking to take some time off before starting, or taking some time off during school. If I had my semester off to do over, I would have done a volunteer program abroad like my friend who went to Africa during her gap year. Habitat for Humanity, which I did post–business school in Tanzania, has great global volunteer programs. You can raise money so it doesn't have to be super-expensive. There are a ton of these types of volunteer travel opportunities that you can research online.

Or You Can Hit Pause During School

No one said you have to go straight through. Sometimes it can be helpful to pause for a bit, reevaluate who you are, and remember why you are at college.

One of my best friends at Harvard took time off after freshman year. He'd been a self-described straight arrow throughout high school, believing like the rest of us that doing the "right" things (getting good grades, playing sports, having well-rounded extracurriculars) would guarantee "success." *Success*, of course, was defined as getting into a good college. But his safe and simple worldview was starting to erode by senior year. His parents were going through financial difficulties, which meant that he was on the brink of not being able to stay at his fancy New England private school, and this fancy school seemed increasingly removed from the real world.

He used swimming as a release, trying to work hard and gain success in the pool as a way to keep a grip on success in the world. At the final championship meet, he stepped up onto the block for the last race of his swimming career, because he wouldn't be competing in college. This moment took on massive importance; he had to do his best. He false-started and was disqualified —

a first in his life. He left the pool and headed to the locker room to have a nervous breakdown of sorts, feeling an unprecedented level of shame. His dad caught him outside and said, "I'm so proud of you." Give his dad the gold! After the crowds left, he and his coach snuck back into the pool. Alone, he swam his last race while his coach timed him. It was the fastest of his career. That experience was life changing, he recently told me, in that he realized playing it safe doesn't assure you of anything and you should follow your passions, not for what they can get you but for how they make you feel.

It's what we talked about with follow your bliss: if you do what you love, the rest takes care of itself. After his freshman year at Harvard, he felt he might squander the incredible opportunity if he didn't get grounded in some larger worldview. He didn't want to play it safe. So he followed his heart and took a year off to do City Year. He got up every day, put on his khakis and Timberlands, did group jumping jacks in public, and then headed off to plant a garden at a school, tutor kids, or help at an assisted-living center. He returned to school refreshed and inspired. He had a great time at Harvard, going pre-med, leading hiking trips, singing a capella, and having tons of friends. He's now a surgeon in Boston with a great family. And he finds time to sing in a band with a bunch of other doctors who are nurturing that blissful, musical piece of themselves.

Another friend of mine at Harvard who was pre-med also decided he needed some time off. (Note, pre-med is not a road to burnout. Plenty of my pre-med pals went straight through and

were happy to do so.) This guy was amazing. He had been working as a volunteer emergency medical technician (EMT) with the
local rescue squad. Even when he wasn't working as an EMT, if
he heard sirens or saw an ambulance, his ears perked up like a
dog, and he'd try to head to the scene. He was addicted to helping
people in a crisis. Aware of his passion, he considered going the
medic route as opposed to becoming a doctor. He wasn't sure if
he should stay pre-med. So he spent the summer before junior
year getting trained as a medic out in California and took off
that fall from school to work as a medic in the Watts neighbor-
hood of Los Angeles. He loved it! He returned that winter, full
of great stories and passion for medicine in general. He ended
up becoming a doctor, going to med school at Tulane. He's an
amazing guy, super interesting and committed to helping people
in a way that always reminds me what true commitment to others looks like.

Regardless of when or why you do it, taking time off can be
a very important breather. I've heard of people helping parents sell
textiles, raising money for kids with cleft palates, learning Chinese,
editing soap operas in Mexico … whatever the experience, the life
lessons were immeasurable and worth the risk and confusion of
doing something different. Many, many people do not have college and/or graduate school careers that go from A to Z. And
I'm guessing that if anything's keeping you up at night, it's the
thought that you'll be rejected everywhere and your life may take
some twisting, unclear, mysterious path. It might, and you will
be all the more blessed for it. All of the people I've mentioned in

these stories are successful, interesting folks. Not one would regret taking the road less traveled.

Nothing Is Forever, and Transferring Is Not the End of the World

What if you choose the wrong school and you're miserable? Or what if you change while you're at school and what once seemed right then becomes wrong? Or what if you need to move to a different part of the country to help a sick family member? Or what if you decide that you want to study acting? What if, what if, what if. There are countless reasons why you might want to transfer. Stuff happens.

I actually spent a year and a half at Northwestern before dropping out. Though sad about going there initially, I tried my best to become a happy college freshman: making great dorm friends, enjoying classes, joining crew, pledging tri-Delt. But by winter, I was growing inexplicably sad, like a fog had rolled over me. I spent a lot of time running up the coast of Lake Michigan and making mix tapes (so old-school!) for my high school boyfriend. I got way too skinny, and it was obvious to everyone that something was wrong. My mom initially suggested transferring during spring of my freshman year. I rejected the idea wholeheartedly. Transferring is weird. Perfect, happy college students don't do that. Who would transfer?

As it turns out... I would. But not after going back to Northwestern for sophomore year to give it, well, the old college try. That fall, however, I got sadder and started fading out of life there completely. By the time I went home for Thanksgiving, I had dropped all of my activities and shut out most of my friends. I couldn't see myself staying at Northwestern, but I couldn't see myself going anywhere else, either. I felt sad and scared and trapped and totally alone in this unnamed battle.

Thanksgiving break involved a bit of drama, including me running away from our Thanksgiving dinner after I called my mom sexist for asking me instead of my brothers to put rolls on the table. Let's just say, I was a mess all weekend. By the time Mom took me to the airport to return to Northwestern on Sunday, I was in hysterics. She let me change my flight and stay home for one more night. And, she told me I could stay home after winter break to think things through. But, she said, I had to go back first, take my finals, and finish the quarter. She knew that only by fully completing that chapter would I create space for a new beginning. Go Mom!

The point of my sharing this melodrama is that you are not trapped. Nothing needs to be forever. You always have choices. In fact, going to two different schools can be really fun. You experience two different types of social lives or parts of the country. Really, the more experiences you have in life, the better. Also, when I restarted at Harvard, people were eager to welcome someone new into the social fold. You'll know yourself better, too, at your second school and can jump right in.

But first you need to get in! Transferring is a slightly different beast than applying the first time around. Schools expect you to know yourself better and to have specific reasons for wanting to transfer. You need to explain how the school you're leaving differs from the one to which you're applying—size, geography, culture, and ideally some academic interest that you can't fulfill at the current school. As I mentioned before, I applied to transfer to Harvard, Brown, Wesleyan, and Bowdoin. They were all smaller, on the East Coast, and more liberal (whatever that means); they all had no fraternity and sorority scene (again, nothing wrong with it—it's just not for all of us); and they all had full women's studies majors, which Northwestern did not at the time.

In helping other folks with transfer applications, I've found that all are able to identify academic reasons for their needing to change—wanting to major in Russian, leaving engineering for liberal arts, or needing smaller class sizes. You need to be slightly more serious academically as a transfer, because you should know why you're leaving one school and going to another.

It's also nice for transfer schools to see that you've given it a try at your first school in the broadest sense. My activities profile at Northwestern (crew, tri-Delt, tutoring) was not as developed as my high school profile (captain of field hockey and swimming, choir and chamber singers, musical and talent show, founded a tutoring program), but it was clear that I was still trying to be me and get involved. Of course, grades matter, too. I had a 3.5 at Northwestern trending upwards, same as in high school. However, if something is not consistent about your profile, you should know what to do after reading chapter 3 on the essays—just explain it to them!

Of course, the essays are key. You need to show how you've

grown up and articulate what lessons you've learned. Changing schools is a big, bold move. In addition to explaining in great detail why this new school would be a better fit, you need to tell them how you've changed and matured since starting college. Think about it from the transfer school admissions committee's perspective — they need to trust that you know what you want better than you did the first time around. And, of course, you need to be your authentic, genuine Self!

One note of caution: try not to start college with the intention of transferring. It's hard to get invested and really give a college a chance if you've already got one foot out the door. Same goes for jobs, people, cities, and everything else new you come across on your path. On that note, let's talk about keeping an open mind as you start school.

Keep Your Mind and Eyes Open to Do What's Best For You

Whether your path is very clear or a bit murky, this process from the essays to the decisions to starting school is about learning how to be honest and make decisions for yourself. Again, take the rejections and acceptances as information, and practice deciding what you should do based on what you feel, what you want, and what you already know deep down within you. How this plays out can look very different from how you imagined it would. There again is the beauty of nonattachment: you're open to following what your heart knows is best for you.

It's so helpful to absorb this lesson of things not looking the way you imagined before you started school, because the truth is, college won't look exactly as you've imagined it. That doesn't mean it will be better or worse than your daydreams, just different. It will be what it is. The beginning, especially, will seem as if you've landed on the moon, because everything is unfamiliar and it can take a bit to find your way.

About a week after arriving at Northwestern, I received a letter from my oldest brother Danny. (I know, no email—can you imagine?) This letter from my big brother was so important and life-saving that I still have it. Here's a bit of his valuable and always witty advice:

> Take those first few weeks of school for what they are—joke material for the next few years, like "and then remember after you shotgunned that six-pack of Natty Light and that cheeseball asked if he could give you a backrub and you puked over his shoulder down the back of his Cherry Garcia shirt? That was so funny!"

Note, I was not shotgunning beers in high school or at Northwestern! Anyway, Danny knew that the beginning of college can be really strange and lonely no matter where you are, even at your dream school. Trust me when I say that all of college won't look like the beginning, and the tough times really do become joke material. (And, dudes, not to belabor the point, but again note the mocking of the guy offering back rubs in your freshman dorm. Heed my warnings!)

Often, we push up against our realities, resisting what's right before us rather than just flowing with it. I never let Northwestern have a chance. I clung to my high school boyfriend, distracted myself by getting too skinny, and didn't open myself up to the place. What a fool. I had great friends, and it's a great school. If I'd gotten over some image of what I thought college should be, maybe I would have loved it there. But I was probably just suffering a bit too much inside on a personal level and may have imploded no matter where I'd started at that time. Tough to say. And, like the people I mentioned, my semester off and transferring was an extremely important time in my life, showing me that I could veer off the typical course, take charge of my life, and make changes. But it's good to keep an open mind for a bit before running away from someplace. We often turn away from the very things and places that might be helpful to us. Before you go and once you're at college, try to drop your image of what things should look like and be present to your reality. Then you can make decisions based on who you actually are and what you really need.

Your life's journey started long before you began applying to college and will go on long after. Every experience, the glorious acceptances and gross rejections in all their forms, will help you live bigger and shine brighter. All you need to do is stay in the moment, see how you feel, and keep it real. As the saying goes, it's not what happens to you in life that defines you, it's your reactions to it. You are always in charge of you.

✦ ✦ ✦

Now that you're choosing your steps on your path, let's talk about how you make your way.

CHAPTER 7

❖

A To-Do List for Higher Level Living

Five Outward Actions and Five Inward Ideas

I t takes a bit of work to live bigger and shine brighter. It requires some awareness of what you're trying to do and how you're doing it. Being your authentic, highest Self in the world is not for the lazy and faint of heart. Buddhists say we're fortunate to be born human because only in human form, as opposed to poodle or fish form, can we grow in our spiritual understandings. Deep, if you think about it: being a human, with the ability to watch your thoughts and feel your heart, gives you the chance consciously to get to know that higher high inside of you. Game on!

In trying to play a little deeper in the spirituality pool, you're becoming more conscious of how you move about in the world, seeing what you know and don't know. You're constantly observing new physical and mental patterns and seeing what you can slough off to reveal your Self. As Pulitzer-winning historian Will Durant (1926, 76) summarized Aristotle's teachings, "We are what we repeatedly do. Excellence, therefore, is not an act; it is a habit." It takes diligence then, constantly paying attention to your actions and your footprint, trying to grow and show your Self.

Our man from last chapter, Sakyong Mipham, the Buddhist scholar in the flowing robes and Ray-Bans, points out just how much effort is involved in the spiritual life. He (2004, 180–81) says, "So much of what passes as spirituality these days is really about pleasure seeking.… This self-absorption disguised as spirituality only leads to more suffering. Real spirituality is about getting grounded. Once we understand who we are, we can realize the needs of others and do something about helping them. Being grounded in who we are is known as basic goodness."

Ah, so the spiritual path is not about simply navel gazing but instead involves serious work to find that innate goodness and grace inside you and do your work to spread it in the world. Otherwise, you're just getting self-absorbed and attached to how enlightened you are while suffering from the pride and ego around that attachment. Also, remember that your work in the world here does not necessarily mean your vocation but living your highest high in each moment so that you are helping those around you in the way only you can.

It can all seem very loosey-goosey, but yoga philosophy gives us directions on living in the world: five ideas that can help us in our outward actions in the world and five ideas to help us deepen inside. Don't you love a list? The MBA in me loves getting a list of yoga philosophy to-dos! Let's check them out.

Five Outward Actions in the World

1. Don't Harm Others or Yourself

Duh. You knew the peace-loving yogis would say we shouldn't beat the pants off each other. In addition to not throwing fisticuffs, nonharming is the idea that we give peace a chance in our hearts and minds. It's about letting things go rather than stewing in anger, which leaves you hurting more than the subject of your rage.

And there are so many chances to let things go in this process of applying to schools—parents may bug, admissions committees may not take awesome you, they may take your awesome best friend instead. You can get very stuck in anger, and the only person who suffers is you. Ralph Waldo Emerson is widely quoted as having said, "For every minute you are angry, you lose sixty seconds of happiness." Or what if you're mad at someone specifically? That will really drag you down. According to the Buddha, holding on to anger is like grasping a hot coal with the intent of throwing it at someone else; you are the one who gets burned. Think about that. It's so true right? You're mad at your parents or a friend or a significant other, and you stew all day about it—who's suffering? You! The best thing to do with anger is just take a breath and put a little space there. It will help just to let it go.

One time when we were kids, we were messing around before

school in the morning and annoying our already exhausted mom. Then the TV announced that we had a snow day. My brothers were so excited they started swinging their backpacks at each other, and one of them hit the fish tank, which broke. Nightmare. My mom's reaction: she walked out the front door to take a breath. Genius. The best part, though, was in doing so, she locked herself out of the house. Ha! We let her back in (after a few moments), but I think all parties benefited from the space! Time and space will help you just let things go. You will feel worlds better.

But we also get angry with ourselves. What about when the anger is turned inside? Quick road to depression, my friends, and I have run down it. Try, try, try to stop beating yourself up for not getting into schools, not doing perfectly on a test, or not scoring with that penalty kick. It happened. It's done. Stay present and move on. Sometimes though, there's no specific event that causes us to harm ourselves; we just tell really negative stories in our own minds about our unworthiness or incompetence or whatever. "I always mess up math tests." "I never make the shot." "I should be taller (or bigger or smaller)." "I'm bad at relationships." "My family is the most messed up." Blah, blah, blah. Some of the deepest violence we do is to our sweet little selves with our crazy, whip-cracking minds. Easy, easy. Back off and give yourself a break. You're creating your reality. Let it be a loving place in your head. Don't harm yourself in thought, word, or deed. Don't harm others in thought, word, or deed. Take a couple of breaths and just let it go.

2. Be Honest and Truthful in What You Say and Do

I was at a party once, and one of my guy friends, trying to be funny, told another woman there he was a fighter pilot (he wasn't). Later, she heard him talking about his office job and said, "Oh my God, you're a liar. You lied to me. You're a liar." Everyone started laughing in this uncomfortable way because when, since second grade, have you heard someone say, "You're a liar"? But she clowned him. She made him look like a total fool for having made her play the fool in his joke with his buddies. No one thought it was an issue, though, until she said something. That's because we lie all the time—we exaggerate our actions, we gossip about others, we pretend to be something we're not.

But think about how you feel when you do that stuff—ugly, right? As John Keats says in "Ode to a Grecian Urn," "Beauty is truth, truth beauty." Word. It just feels gross when you're not being truthful. According to Eboo Patel in his fascinating book *Acts of Faith: The Story of an American Muslim, the Struggle for the Soul of a Generation* (2007, 107), the Prophet Mohammed said, "God is beautiful and loves beauty." *God, beauty, truth, beauty, God*... these words all seem to flow nicely together for a reason. Your beautiful highest Self is a truthful one.

That's all very lofty and nice, but let's get practical. Don't lie about yourself to make yourself look good and don't lie about others to make yourself look better than them. Lies backfire, and you end up feeling bad and looking lame. As we discussed in chapter 1, the whole application process is just begging for gossip. But put on your bigger person suit, sashay around in that, and don't talk smack. It's a good habit to get into before you get to college. Remember the warnings not to be the dude offering back rubs in the freshman dorm? Same deal. No one likes the classmate talking trash about other people. Look, even if the garbage you're spewing is true, reference nonviolence and don't do harm to others. Just zip it and focus on living your life. Let your reputation be based on your actions, not lame stories about other people. And remember, karmically, that gossip will come back around your way. Yowza.

3. Don't Steal From Others

Again, this seems like a no-brainer, right? Don't take people's stuff. We learned that in nursery school, and hopefully that's been working out for you. But there's more that you can steal. Obviously, not stealing words and ideas is big when you're writing essays and later when you're in college. Keep it clean and do your work. In the interest of not stealing words, I'll quote Nischala Joy Devi from an interview in *Yoga Journal* (Dowdle 2009, 80): "There are lots of things you can steal.... You can steal someone's time if you are late. You can steal someone's energy. You can steal someone's happiness. You can steal someone else's ideas if you represent them as your own."

It's a stressful time for you right now, so just watch if you're getting a little shady because of the competition. For example, how about this whacked-out college stress story? During spring of sophomore year, I ran for reelection as class officer. I had served as sophomore class officer with two guys, and it was supposed to be an easy election for all of us. So I was surprised when they were reelected but I wasn't. Though a competitive kid, I wasn't too upset. I was busy with other stuff and a little tired of one of the guys. Then one afternoon as I left choir, a classmate I didn't know that well pulled me into the empty ceramics room. Kinda creepy. He told me that the guy who'd defeated me, a seemingly laid-back artsy type, had rigged the election to win. He'd stuffed the ballot box or something. How was that even possible? The artsy dude figured I had enough going for me on my college applications and he needed the class officer position more. My brain could hardly comprehend such dishonesty. It probably wasn't even true, but just the thought freaked me out. It freaked me out that someone would be so sleazy just to improve his resume. So just check yourself before you karmically wreck yourself; don't mess things up in the name of looking better for schools.

Also, if things aren't going well for you, like say you just got rejected from your dream school, it can be easy to rain on the parade of your friend who just got accepted to her dream school. Don't steal her joy. Celebrate with her instead. You'll feel worlds better. Nonstealing is also about not coveting what others have, basically checking your jealousy at the door and not bringing it into your precious Self. Nothing (nothing!) makes you feel worse than jealousy. Talk about instant karma. Comparing yourself or wanting what others have is the fast road to misery. Live your life. Cultivate gratitude for what you have and the lessons you get, and awesomeness will flow your way.

Okay, bear with me on this next one. Energy thieving sounds hoo-hah, but it's all around us. Be aware of what you're giving in relationships, and don't be afraid to give yourself some space from people who just suck you dry. That sounds airy-fairy, but you know what I'm talking about; some people deplete you. Don't let yourself get dragged down by others, and don't do the dragging yourself.

Finally, this nonstealing can also speak to your footprints on the planet. The first step is not taking more than you need and trying your best to put things back. We're all looking at this in a big way these days, as we green up our acts. But you can look at this from the perspective of the college admissions process, too. For example, don't apply to a million schools just to rack up acceptances while creating rejections or wait-list situations for people who really love those schools. Overall, this concept of nonstealing is about watching what you put out and what you take back and having gratitude for all that's in your world.

4. Focus on What's Important

I love this lesson on staying focused (she writes as she changes the song on her iTunes, checks her email, and then returns to the sentence at hand). Sigh. One of my favorite yoga teachers describes this idea as not frittering away our energy. We're big fritterers, aren't we? Always doing a zillion things at once and usually none of them very well. Your math teacher was onto something when she told you that you'd learn the material if you actually paid attention in class.

Okay, so there are some obvious applications of nonfrittering to your life now and at college. While you're applying, there's a lot on your plate. Take a step back, look at what is really important to you, and put your efforts there. It goes back to my annoying bike-riding advice to my nephew of meeting your fatigue with effort instead of with distraction and wasted time. When you're working on your applications, do it—work on your essays and put your focus there. When you're waiting to hear from schools, try not to waste your energy worrying; we've discussed this (in chapter 6), and it will get you nowhere. Be in the present instead and focus on the big fun and discovery that is second semester senior year. If you don't get into the schools you want, then just take a breath, do some thinking, and make a plan. Freaking out, as I did with melodramatic storming out of the house, is *so* not productive. Give yourself a moment or a month, and then think about what you truly want to do.

And once you're at college, you'll be tempted to sign up for every club, and if you need a semester or two of being spread thin to figure out what you love and care about, then that's cool. But then try to focus on the things that bliss you out so you can develop leadership and experience in those areas. Plus, you want to leave yourself some energy for hanging out and just being in college. *But!* Don't waste your energy on people, things, or pursuits that aren't helping you grow. You know that stuff that just drags you down or the people who make you feel bad about yourself? Kiss it all good-bye and shine your light elsewhere.

5. Don't Cling to Anyone, Anything, or Any Idea

This idea already has come up a bunch of times because it's super important. We tend to grab onto everything that's in front of us: people, clothes, food, fantasies. We want and want and cling and cling. You know that feeling when you're grasping or clinging to dreams or people or memories. OMG, it is the worst. In Tibetan Buddhism, one of the real bummer forms, unlike the human form capable of deepening spirituality, is the hungry ghost. Sounds like a bad time already, right? The hungry ghosts have these big empty bellies, open mouths, and skinny necks, and they can never get enough. They want and want and want. I've read that they love with possessiveness, clinging and wanting something or someone to be theirs versus loving them but letting them be their own person. And if you have ever been in a relationship where you were hanging onto someone who just wasn't right for you and they were treating you badly, then you know what we're talking about here. We also cling to habits, fearful of shedding them to start a new life. We cling to ideas of the future, afraid of existing in the present. All of that clinging will take you down, man.

You've got nothing to give the world if you're hanging onto stuff. Let it go and instead open yourself to the yumminess that will enter when you're open and receptive. This is big when you head off to college. You'll want to bring so much of your old life with you, from pictures to relationships to preconceptions of your-self and college life, and it can really drag you down. Now you don't want to cut ties just for the sake of cutting them, but let yourself be ready for the new stuff that's right there, ready for you to enjoy.

In letting go, you lose nothing. Life's so much easier when you stop the work of grasping and instead open yourself up to receive.

✦ ✦ ✦

So those are the ideas to live by in terms of moving about in the world: nonharming, truthfulness, nonstealing, conserving energy, and nongrasping. If they are all starting to meld together, that's good. It means you're getting the overall schtick of releasing from fearful human behavior and opening up to your faith-filled Self. You can start becoming more conscious of what's difficult for you and stepping into challenges that let you grow, advancing up the rungs of earth school.

Five Inward Ideas

Let's check out the things to strive for as you do some work from the inside out.

1. Keep It Clean

This is not about being squeaky clean or eating like a bunny (although showering will make you more popular, and veggies do a body good). This idea of cleanliness, or purity, is similar to what we talked about around self-care in chapters 4 and 5. Again, you want to recognize all of the "food" you're taking in—conversation, media, actual food, exercise, emotions. You are not only what you eat but what you do, read, and listen to and whom you hang around, watch, and think about. What you put in you becomes you at a cellular level. You take on the energy that's around you. (And here goes the feather-skirt-chakra talk.) Seriously, this is about having awareness of and making conscious choices as to what goes into your mind, body, and soul. Are your choices helping you become more open or more closed?

Starting with the application process, you can choose how you spend your time and invest your energy and what you take in. Perhaps most important, you can choose what emotions you entertain — envy and pride or gratitude and charity, stress and panic or curiosity and faith. Know that it will take some time to build up the gratitude, charity, curiosity, and faith muscles in your brain if you've hard-wired yourself to stress and panic. This again is about letting yourself get still and listening to your heart, which is *so* not interested in stress and panic. Then as you head off to school and make choices about what your days look like, how you spend your time, and how you live your life, you can get a clear picture of how what you consume (on every level) affects you. Don't worry about being squeaky-clean Captain Purity, but you can make grown-up decisions about clearing garbage out of your life and feeling good instead.

2. Cultivate Contentment

Biggie alert, biggie alert! This is serious joy-in-the-journey work here. But sometimes it's hard to know if contentment is an action or a result. We've chatted about how the happiness we gain from satisfying our desires is only fleeting. You are momentarily happy, but then you are left with emptiness as you long for the next object of desire. Whereas by bringing an attitude of contentment to all of your activities, you will not hold expectations; thus, you will be satisfied and happy no matter what the outcome. This happiness is true and lasting bliss. But sometimes in going for the lasting happiness, we stop ourselves from even experiencing the fleeting happiness because we're already anticipating the happiness deflation. That's when the anticipation of a goal is sweeter than the reward.

Gradually, we can practice an absence of expectations to be content with any and all outcomes of our actions. This is truly embracing the process of life and feeling joy in the journey, no matter what it brings. However, this active contentment requires serious discipline to retrain the brain after years of being very externally achievement oriented, competitive, and hard on ourselves (or at least it does for me!). You can't just flip a switch and say, "I'm going to be grateful now." Instead, at those moments when you are angry and jealous and thinking that everyone gets a break but you… that's the teachable moment when you've got to school yourself to step back and brainstorm what you're grateful for. Crazy hard. Yet after a while, it becomes more natural to go to gratitude mode, whether things are going well or not.

A friend and I were chatting about faith recently, and he said that the one danger in being so faith filled is that you're disappointed by the world more. But it's just the opposite. You're looking for the lessons, the gifts, the moments for gratitude, and as a result, you don't see the grossness quite so much. There's that great quote from Wayne Dyer (2007, 74): "When you change the way you look at things, the things you look at change." The more you work to follow the light-filled energy in your life and heart, the brighter your world will become.

3-4-5. Discipline, Reflection, Devotion

These three go together like chocolate, peanut butter, and ... maybe more chocolate? They are really just a review of what you're practicing. Becoming the highest, best, most genuine, love-filled, forgiving, faithful version of you is not child's play, though kids do seem to be better at this than grown-ups because they haven't yet covered themselves up in protective armor of fear, sarcasm, and skepticism. But just like kids, and I'm thinking of my third graders, we all respond well to structure. Having some order and discipline on our path actually sets us free to feel, live, and love as we were meant to. Adding some space between you and your thoughts, being present, releasing attachments ... this all may seem very difficult, but the more you train your mind to work in service of your heart, the easier life will be. You will have to discipline yourself and do the heavy lifting, but doing so will make your load lighter.

As you make your way, the reflection or self-study starts to become second nature. That witness part of you is ready and waiting to help your Self emerge. You'll evaluate your actions, choices, thoughts, and feelings. You'll see your patterns for what they are, just habits, and begin to make decisions about who you are and how you want to live in the world. You can separate from fearful human behavior and leave some room for your natural, loving Self to dance about.

Self-study also means looking at what you're putting into yourself in terms of inspiration, texts, and information. Let yourself seek out teachers, books, and friends that help you become more of your Self. You will know what people, things, and situations feed your love and authenticity. Follow that energy.

In the end, let yourself settle into the mystery of life and explore devotion towards the grace that helps us all get by. Who is to know what we are all doing here? So it's best just to do our best and offer up the results. That's all we can do really. Try our hardest to recognize lessons, learn them, and grow into a fuller expression of who we are. Know that you're in it to win it with the rest of us; we're all just drops in the sea of humanity floating about. It can be beautiful to consider that we're all so small yet part of the massive bigness that's out there. We can all learn from and teach each other as we practice being present, becoming our true Selves, and letting go to find joy in the journey.

✦ ✦ ✦

You get this joy-in-the-journey stuff. No more big messages to hammer home. The wrap-up's just for fun.

FINAL THOUGHTS

❖

Joy in the Journey

At Harvard, I was a leader for the First-year Outdoor Program trips (FOP). You've probably heard of these types of orientation outings. You spend a week before school hiking, canoeing, or doing some such outdoorsy thing with a small group of first years and upperclassman leaders. Wicked good time! I didn't do a FOP trip as a first year at Harvard because, of course, I spent my first year at Northwestern. Though there I did a cool urban volunteering program, which is another excellent orientation option at most schools. Anyway, having done an Outward Bound trip during my time off from school, I applied to be a FOP leader and was thrilled to be selected. My FOP leader-training trip at the end of sophomore year was one of my favorite times at Harvard. I met my best friend Rach, scrambled up peaks, gazed out over treetops, learned how to treat heat exhaustion and sprains, and delighted at watching our dashing British friend become very

uncomfortable when the California gals and a hippie Massachu-
setts dude went skinny-dipping.

I was psyched, albeit a bit nervous about the responsibility,
to lead my first FOP trip before the start of my junior year. I was
paired up with a senior guy whom I didn't know. He was a tall,
athletic, ROTC type. Classically Harvard, in my eyes. When the
steering committee announced that we would be leading the hard-
est-level trip up the Presidential section of the White Mountains,
he pumped his fists and screamed, "Yeeeeeeaaaaaahhhhhhh!" Lest
I think he found *me* that exciting, he explained that he was fired
up to get the most physically challenging trip. Being a bit of a
jock, the hiking didn't scare me—but he kinda did. Together, we
set about planning our specific route for the five-day hike. He
was way intense but also disarmingly childlike in his enthusiasm
for planning a really aggressive trip. I followed his lead because
he had more FOP experience and, well, it didn't seem like I had
a choice in the matter.

Our FOPpers, which is the cute term for the first-year trip
participants, were indeed adorable. I don't mean to sound conde-
scending. But when you get to college, you're nervous and shy and
eager to make friends—you're adorable. We spent our first night
together in an empty dorm room practicing for tight tarp living,
dividing up the food, breaking the ice, and discussing the route.
A few of them looked a little nervous about being on the hard-
est-level trip. I assured them it was no big deal, and my coleader
assured them it was going to kick some serious ass.

The next morning, we drove up to New Hampshire and hit

the trail. After a couple of hours of hiking, it started raining and feeling much more like early fall than end of summer. Of course, we'd looked at the weather reports and knew it would be little rainy at the beginning of the trip. At home, my parents were hearing the Weather Channel talk of severe thunderstorms sweeping through western New Hampshire right where their baby was leading 12 other parents' babies up Mount Washington.

By late afternoon, the rain got heavy, and the wind picked up big-time. Our adorable FOPpers stoically suited up in their newly purchased rain gear. We were a parade of goofballs in GORE-TEX, except the blonde from Seattle who looked totally runway in her well-fitted, worn-in gear and waterproof cowgirl hat. The group's requisite tough guy started acting pretty obnoxious, even for a tough guy, and said some strange, violent stuff. As newly minted wilderness first-aid responders, my coleader and I knew that weird behavior was a sign of prehypothermia. But we chalked it up to tough guy bravado overdrive and decided just to keep an eye on him. Then he started tripping easily and looking pale, also signs of prehypothermia. We stopped to check him out, and he immediately fell to the ground in the fetal position, shaking hard.

Within moments, we had a tarp set up to block the rain and set about undressing and then redressing him in the warmest, driest gear we had. The other FOPpers rocked: making sure the tarp was secure, lighting the stove for hot drinks, and averting their eyes as the coleaders pulled clothes off of their cocky classmate. As soon as he was warm and dry and drinking hot lemonade, our tough guy perked up, got some color back, and generally looked and felt great. But the whole ordeal was freaking terrifying. We spent the night right there, struggling to keep the stove lit in the wind as we made dinner and then huddling together sleepless under the tarp as the sky unleashed torrents of rain on us.

In the morning, we were met with gray skies but no rain. As we packed up, we checked out the damage of soaking wet clothes and sleeping bags. We were scheduled to do a hard-core hike along the top of a ridge that day and were close enough to the location that we still could. I pulled my coleader into a private chat and said I didn't think it was a good idea to do the ridge climb, which he *really* wanted to do. I pointed out that our prehypothermic guy had been, well, prehypothermic, and we needed to dry our stuff, especially our sleeping bags. He nodded and then turned to the group and put it to a vote: who was tough and wanted to do the ridge walk, and who was a pansy? The guys tentatively put up their hands to being tough. The women raised their hands to being pansies. It was a draw. My coleader started arguing how amazing the ridge walk would be. But my inner mama bear emerged, and I put my foot down. No ridge walk. Crown me Queen Pansy.

Instead, we found a cabin on the map and hiked there to spend the rest of the day trying to dry out our stuff. Once at the cabin, we hung up our clothes and bags, made hot cocoa, sang songs, and danced around like fools. I led the singing and dancing while my coleader took a nap. It was a great day. After 24 hours with forced stripping, crazy rainstorms, Queen Pansy throwdown, and now some getting down, we were super bonded.

Though our emotions were warmed up, our gear was still

cold and wet, as cloudy New Hampshire skies don't do much for drying things out. After waking up from his nap, my coleader surveyed the scene and declared things to be "much worse than they seemed." He decided he should walk alone up to the nearby Appalachian Mountain Club hut to figure out a plan. Having two older brothers, I know how guys get when they're hungry, so we gave him some peanuts and M&M's and he chilled. Together, he and I decided that we'd all spend the night there and as a group go to the AMC hut in the morning. But we only had six dry sleeping bags for 12 people. We told the FOPpers we'd have to sleep two-to-a-bag to stay warm. My coleader and I would share a bag. The super-cute dude offered a space in his dry bag to the blonde from Seattle. Well played, dude. The rest also paired up guy-gal. Maybe the FOPpers weren't so nervous and shy after all.

In the morning, we packed up and hiked toward the AMC hut at Lakes of the Clouds, which had not been on our original route. It wasn't an easy hike, and it got increasingly misty as we got higher. The lack of visibility inspired us all to get very quiet, focusing on putting foot in front of foot. Gradually, we heard a gentle lapping sound. When we lifted our heads, as if on cue, the mist let up to reveal a completely still lake right before us, appearing to float literally in the clouds. We stopped. It was breathtaking.

Just around the side of the lake, we saw the AMC hut, which was a huge relief. When we arrived, a staff member and a few other hikers were hanging out. They generously welcomed us, and the FOPpers settled into peanut butter sandwiches and slices of cheese. Good living. My coleader went into excellent logistics action mode, calling our base camp to explain the situation. He told them we couldn't continue with wet sleeping bags and made a plan for us to hike down Tuckerman's Ravine, where the base team would meet us with a van. He figured out a safe, clear route for us to take down the mountain. And that's what we did.

On the day that we were supposed to be summitting Mount Washington, we were instead drying out our clothes and sleeping bags at a laundromat, all of us very happy to do so. My coleader, in fact, settled into being a great leader himself of singing and nonsense. We spent that night at a local car camping area and restarted our ascent in the morning. We still had a couple good days of hiking after that and even reached a peak or two, but it was a different trip. We were humbled, and our route was a lot less aggressive than what we had planned.

The blonde from Seattle and the super-cute dude were clearly on their way to being a couple by the end of the trip (and were still going strong two years later when I graduated). The tough, hypothermic guy ended up being very sweet and warm, no pun intended. Many of the women who voted for the pansy option proved to be very strong, brave hikers, surprising themselves. On the last night, we shared our thoughts over the traditional FOP cheesecake ritual. You circle up and feed a bite to the person next to you while you say something you like about him or her. Oh, FOP cuteness. As with any trip, our FOPpers expressed admiration and respect and love for each other, and we ate up our inside jokes.

Of course, I don't know what personal lessons each FOPper

learned. Similarly, I can't speak to what my coleader took away. But he gave me props for standing up to him, apologized for freaking out, and complimented me on keeping the FOPpers' spirits up. It takes a big man to admit when he's messed up a bit, and his bigger person suit fit very well. I gave him return props on rallying to be an excellent partner, sharp with logistics, full of solutions, and capable of spectacular silliness. I'll be forever grateful to him for using his leadership to get us down the mountain and out of a wet, cold situation. Over the course of that week, I learned to be much more confident and assertive and trust that I do know things. I also gained respect for my natural soft skills in helping people feel at ease. Maybe most important, I had spent my first year at Harvard feeling a little intimidated, and that trip made me realize that my attitude was foolish and fearful. I entered junior year ready to spread my wings.

We could have climbed Mount Washington. We would have had glorious lessons learned from reaching the top, though we wouldn't have seen the heavenly Lakes in the Clouds or discovered our inner reserves of humility and flexibility. The end place on the map wasn't the point at all. Our purpose that week was to become friends, learn about ourselves, discover new strengths, and shed limiting weaknesses. The point wasn't conquering a mountain and getting a bigger view from the top; rather, the reward was connecting with each other and deepening the view of our Selves within.

The journey is *so* the reward—on a mountain, in high school, throughout college, and forever more.

You're Accepted

You can let this application process be the beginning of a beautiful journey to follow your bliss and reveal the real you. It's not an easy journey, uncovering your Self, and it requires effort and release, strength and surrender. But if you pay attention and learn your lessons, your life will unfold in a glorious way. It will be more spectacular than you could ever imagine.

When the student is ready, the teacher appears. So let this process of applying to college be your teacher. Let this rite of passage into adulthood teach you this profound truth: you can love and accept yourself in each moment simply for being you. And then take your fine, fabulous, faith-filled Self out for a spin and celebrate the glory that is your unique heart and soul.

I hope that my experience and words have helped you out a little bit. Though we haven't met, of course, I'm rooting for you to be fearless, play it big, and find the joy in the journey of your precious life. I'll leave you the way we leave yoga classes, with the word *namaste*. It's a Sanskrit word that means "the divine within me sees the divine within you." It's a powerful way to walk through the world, looking for that light in others and radiating it from yourself. Know that you've always got that divine light in you. Let it shine out for the whole world to see. *Namaste.*

Namaste

It is with my deepest gratitude that I acknowledge the many people who helped me along this journey, and I don't just mean the book. Apologies in advance from this first time author for a gratuitously long acknowledgments section, but I am thrilled to publicly thank those who have touched my heart.

First, I am so grateful for Ryan Fischer-Harbage, my heart-filled super agent. I thank you for your commitment to this idea and your faith in me. Because you believed I could do this, I started to see it was possible. I told you that if this book never happened, I would be content to simply have gained you as a friend. I meant that. The book's gravy.

I offer a tremendous thank you to Don Fehr, my editor at Kaplan, who immediately understood and encouraged my take on the application process. Your perseverance made the college book a reality, and I will be forever grateful to you for that. Also thank you for always following up any suggestions with a reminder that this was my book.

I want to thank all of Kaplan for taking good care of my book and me. Thank you to Susan Barry for calm and wise leadership, Rachel Bergman for keeping so many moving parts together,

Julio Espin for explaining how a book comes to be, and Tim Brazier for navigating the public relations world (and coming to yoga class!).

Ruth Mills took great care in editing this work and she had a big job to do with this rookie writer. Thank you for doing the heavy lifting and helping me find a structure that worked for all of my stories and information.

Thank you to Paula Fleming for an excellent copy edit and for being so careful with my thoughts and intentions.

For the past few years I was able to create a viable life as a yoga teacher and admissions consultant because of Stacy Blackman. Stacy, it was an honor to help you with the tremendous growth of Stacy Blackman Consulting. I admire you so much for your balance of professionalism and compassion. I consider you a true mentor and great friend.

Everyone in my world has heard me sing the praises of Kimberly Salshutz, my acupuncturist. Kimberly, you are my guru of healing and hope. Thank you for helping me believe in the beautiful possibilities coming my way. Your encouragement and faith were invaluable to my creating this book. You are one of the biggest blessings in my life.

Mary Kuentz, coach extraordinaire, you coached the book proposal right out of me. I am so grateful for your love and insight, and your good teachings around gifts, values, balance and obstacles. The ripple effect of your extraordinary work is unending and the world is a better place because you walk through it, sister!

I put my hands to my heart in gratitude for Oliver Ryan who fortuitously happened into my yoga class just as I began writing this book. Oliver, you have been a precious and cherished source of warmth, humor, and moral support. I hope you recognize your advice and our conversations scattered throughout these pages. Thank you for being my best friend during this time in my life as well as my writing coach and my very first sale.

I am overflowing with love and gratitude for my community at the Yoga Works downtown studio in New York. Thank you to my students for always coming to class with effort, heart, and humor. It is my great privilege to learn from you and such a joy to share the practice. And I am so touched that you have cheered me on with the book. Amy Benson, thanks for making me feel like I was in the writer's club; I'm so envious of *your* students. Sarah Carl, thanks for cover and subtitle help and generally helping me feel like a real author. A special thank you to Jenny Aurthur for seeing the yoga teacher in me (before I even did) and for continuing to encourage me on this path. Also, thank you to Carrie Owerko at the Iyengar Institute for helping me take my practice to new levels. A huge heart-filled shout out to my Yoga Works teacher-friend-peeps who have given me much love over the years: Chrissy Carter, Jodie Rufty, Tzahi Moskovitz, Susan Lippy Orem, Jeanmarie Paolillo, Paula Lynch, Arana Shapiro, Julie Marx, Janna Siegel, Edwin Bergman, Cleandra Martin, Christy Allen, Jennie Cohen, and Keith Yzquierdo.

Massive thank you to my friends for being fantastic cheerleaders. I'm so grateful to those of you who shared your stories for this book: Missy Ross, Elizabeth Dowling, Katherine Fausset, Vanessa Coke, Sarah Aviram, Karen Aviram, Kristin

Resnansky, Moire Kenney, Romesh Ratnesar, Matthew Tripp, Kiki Fair, Oliver Ryan, and especially Matt Carty who characteristically opened his heart and will touch countless others in doing so. Many more friends are dancing through these pages as very anonymous examples, and it was so nice to think about you all as I wrote this.

Tons of love and gratitude to my girls from over the years who have always supported my twists and turns: Missy Ross, Jessica Sankey, Rachel Garlin, Mehana Blaich, Vanessa Coke, Katherine Fausset, Liz Hammond, Nell Brown, Arielle Guy, Lori Legaspi, Meredith Landers, and Karen Aviram. And, my best man Michael Wertheim. I love you each one of you so, so much.

A special thank you to Kareem Ghalib for having the love and compassion to care for me throughout my tough times at Northwestern and having the maturity and grace to remain a dear friend forever after.

My Most Valuable Guru award goes to Jerry Hauser, my manager/mentor/surrogate big brother from Teach For America. The director of admissions role, applying to Stanford...my best career moves were your idea! Our friendship is one of my favorites, and I thank you for so many thoughtful, hilarious and inspiring talks over the years.

Thank you to Professor Michael Ray from Stanford for pushing my thinking on who is my self and what is my work. Thank you for introducing me to the hero's journey, the coin toss, and the very yogic concept of no expectations. Also thanks for that walk on the beach in Santa Cruz when I came back for reunion.

You are a true guru, helping so many students reach for creative, inspiring lives.

During some of my toughest times over the past decade I have been greatly helped by chatting with Reverend Skip Masback of the Congregational Church of New Canaan, Connecticut. Skip, you are my guru of vocation, and I thank you for helping me follow my bliss. Also you told me once that the timeline for change in my life wasn't mine to control, and I have felt great freedom to simply learn my lessons and enjoy the ride ever since.

I have been blessed to mentor a phenomenal group of students through the Fresh Air Fund. You all have been my inspiration when I stared through tears at my computer wondering if I could or should write this book. I especially want to thank Melanie and Chazz—you are amazing individuals and beautiful writers; please keep putting words on the page because the world needs your voices.

I am so grateful for all of my MBA admissions clients from Stacy Blackman Consulting each of whom became a great friend. It was an honor to hear your stories as you fearlessly answered essay questions from the depths of your hearts. For many obvious reasons, this book could not have happened without you. But most of all, it was in helping you become writers that I decided to give it a try myself. Thank you!

I have a huge, colorful, hilarious extended family that deserves many thanks for their love and support and for being tons of fun. My many aunts and uncles have taken great interest in my various career moves and ideas over the years, and I thank you for believing in me. I am so blessed to have had close relationships with my grandparents: Dan and Viola Malachuk, and Rodney and Isabel Ford. Your stories walk with me everyday. You gave me an invaluable sense of our immigrant history and inspired me to take advantage of educational opportunities and make my dreams come true.

My family has gained two excellent additions over the years thanks to my brother Danny: my beautiful sister-in-law Katie Reinhardt and my awesome nephew Paul. Katie R, thank you for bringing a true sister's support and wisdom to my world. I love you and am grateful for our relationship. Paul, you are in this book so much because I learn so much from you! I am blown away by your love for reading and engineering and science and your talents as a swimmer and singer. I love you and can't wait to see what you bring to the world.

I'm struggling to find the words to express the depth of my love and gratitude for my two older brothers, who are my biggest heroes and greatest fans. Growing up I understood what natural gifts looked like by watching Mike shoot a thousand free throws and pull off reverse dunks, and hearing Danny rip through Jimi Hendrix guitar riffs and play the piano by ear treating us to our *South Pacific* sing-along-favs. I learned the power of words, humor, and stories watching Mike captivate a room as he spun tales to extraordinary heights of hilarity, and reading Danny's brilliant letters from college through my tears of laughter. Also, as a little girl it was a precious gift to have big brothers who openly protected, admired, and adored me so that I understood that boys and men have hearts, feelings, and sensitive souls. As we've become adults, you have become my best friends and greatest teachers. Mike, I admire your resilience and fearless ability to change, and I count on you to be my philosopher king inspiring me to follow my heart. Danny, I admire your fierce intellect and commitment to following your bliss, and I count on you to be my wise and witty professor inspiring me to flex my brain. In terms of this book, you are both experienced authors who lent me valuable counsel. Mike, you helped me to remember the fun in writing and use it as a release. Danny, as always, you helped me to organize my thoughts and go into power tool mode. You both have filled my life with so much love and laughter. We joke that somewhere along the way I became the oldest, but I'd be lost without the two of you.

If it was difficult to express how much I appreciate my brothers, thinking about my parents makes me want to fall to my knees and weep out of love and gratitude. Simply put, I won the life lottery being born to Dan and Ginger Malachuk.

Dad, I thank you for being the ultimate, dutiful dad by loving me, providing for me, and ensuring that I had opportunities far beyond your own. Moreover, I thank you for respecting my choices and dreams as I took risks. You have been my safety net in your steadiness, and also my greatest cheering section in your quiet way of covertly crying when I got into Harvard after dropping out of college, or sending me articles about education policy and school admissions trends, or listening with apparent interest as I discuss yoga. Many years ago at a reunion of the Hilton Head families I overheard you describing with great pride how hard I'd been working as a third grade teacher. When another dad in the crowd asked what I would do after TFA, I heard you say, "Anything she wants." What a lucky girl to have always known that you believed I could do anything. I love you so much.

Mom, our GG, what to say? You gave me the gift of my life. And we have been best friends the whole way through. You have physically, emotionally and spiritually picked me up and sent me back out into the world time and time again. Of the many gifts you have passed down to me from your ridiculous humor to your loving heart to your not so hidden inner performer, I am most grateful that you gave me your rock solid faith. It is you who taught me that trees only grow in the valley and the best is yet to come. I thank you for having the courage to be open about your relationship with God and for having the respect to stand back and let me discover where God talks to me, which is when I'm standing on top of a mountain or on the top of my head. In my lowest of lows a few years ago, when I was planting the seeds for the breakthroughs discussed in this book it is you who told me: "Those who hope in the Lord will renew their strength. They will soar on wings like eagles; they will run and not grow weary, they will walk and not be faint." (Isaiah 40:31). Soar indeed, GG. Thank you for giving me roots and wings.

References

Buechner, Frederick. 1973. *Wishful Thinking: A Theological ABC*. New York: Harper & Row.

Campbell, Joseph. 1990. *The Hero's Journey: Joseph Campbell on His Life and Work*. Ed. Phil Cousineau. New York: Harper & Row.

Campbell, Joseph. 1991. *The Art of Living*. New York: HarperCollins.

de Mille, Agnes. 1991. *Martha: The Life and Work of Martha Graham*. New York: Random House.

Desikachar, T. K. V. 1999. *The Heart of Yoga: Developing a Personal Practice*. Rev. ed. Rochester, Vt.: Inner Traditions.

Dowdle, Hillari. 2009. Ten steps to happiness. *Yoga Journal*, February.

Durant, William. 1926. *The Story of Philosophy: The Lives and Opinions of the World's Greatest Philosophers*. Repr., New York: Simon & Schuster/Pocket Books, 1991.

Dyer, Wayne W. 2007. *Change Your Thoughts, Change Your Life: Living the Wisdom of the Tao*. Carlsbad, Calif.: Hay House.

Easwaran, Eknath, trans. 2007. *The Bhagavad Gita*. 2nd ed. Tomales, Calif.: Nilgiri Press.

Emerson, Ralph Waldo. 1841. Self-reliance. In *Essays* (1841) and *Essays: First Series* (1847). http://www.emersoncentral.com/self reliance.htm.

Goldberg, Natalie. 1986. *Writing Down the Bones: Freeing the Writer Within.* Boston: Shambhala.

Mipham, Sakyong. 2004. *Turning the Mind into an Ally.* New York: Riverhead.

Palmer, Parker J. 1999. *Let Your Life Speak: Listening for the Voice of Vocation.* San Francisco: Jossey-Bass.

Patel, Eboo. 2007. *Acts of Faith: The Story of an American Muslim, the Struggle for the Soul of a Generation.* Boston: Beacon Press.

Rūmī, Jalāl ad-Dīn Muḥammad. 1995. *The Essential Rumi.* Trans. Coleman Barks and John Moyne. New York: HarperCollins. Originally published in the 13th century in Central Asia. http://www.bdancer.com/med-guide/culture/rumi.html.

Waitzkin, Josh. 2007. *The Art of Learning: An Inner Journey to Optimal Performance.* New York: Free Press.

About the Author

Katie Malachuk graduated magna cum laude from Harvard and earned an MBA from Stanford. She has served as director of admissions for Teach For America, developing and managing an admissions process that screened thousands of applicants a year. Since business school, Katie has worked for a top-tier management consulting firm and an education focused start-up enterprise. Most recently she has been highly successful as an MBA admissions consultant and, on a pro bono basis, counsels high school students through the college application process. Katie is a yoga instructor and a certified life coach. She is also the author of *Earn It: A Stress-Free and Proven Approach to Getting into Top MBA Programs*. She can be found at *www.katiemalachuk.com*.

Index

A

Academic life
  course offerings, 30-31
  questions to consider, 32-33
  study abroad programs, 31-32
Acceptance, 256
Admissions committee, 211-12
Ambivalence, 181
Attachment, 103, 113-19
Aversion, 103, 119-29

B

Balance, 148
Blessings, 133
Bliss
  achieving, 57-58
  calling element, 89-97
  explanation of, 57-63
  gift element, 63-77
  vaues element, 77-89
Boredom, 183-85

C

Calling
  finding, 89-97
  inspiration for, 93-94
City/country setting, 12
Cleanliness, 243-44
Club offerings, 17
Coin toss, 46
College counselor, 160-61
College town, 12
Competition
  emotions around, 4, 49-50
  feelings about, 48-52
  reaction to, 48-49
Contentment cultivation, 244-45
Course offerings, 30-33
Critical thinking, 113
Culture, 16-19

D

Decisions, 210-14
Devotion, 246-47
Discipline, 246-47
Diversity, 13-16
Dress, style of, 18

E

Educational debt, 28-29
Ego, 103, 105-13
Emotions, 49-50
Energy exercise, 42-43
Essay
  attachment, 103, 113-19
  authenticity, 143
  aversion, 119-29
  courage, 143
  divergent opinions, 112-13
  ego involvement, 103, 105-13
  fear, 129-31
  fun with, 135-36
  hero's journey model, 122
  honesty, 106-12
  lessons learned, 120-22
  motivations, 142
  outside influences, 117-18
  personal, 118-19

self-discovery, 101-3, 125-29
self-editing, 118-19
topic, 99-100, 137-42
transfer, 227-28
Essay question
    example of you in action, 139-41
    what you want to do in life, 141-42
    who are you, 137-39
Exercise, 179
Exhaustion, 176-80
Extracurriculars
    questions to consider, 25-26
    school choice factors, 5-6, 23-26

F
Faith, 195-202
Fear, 104, 129-31, 195-202
Financial aid
    grants, 28
    questions to consider, 29-30
    school choice factors, 26-30
    work-study programs, 27-28
First thoughts, 133
Focus, 240-41
Fraternities, 17
Friends, 158-59

G
Geography, 8-13
Gifts
    acknowledgment, 65
    channeling to career, 69-71
    discovery exercise, 74-77
    effortless aspect of, 72-73
    nurturing, 77
    uncovering, 73
Grants, 28
Gratitude journal, 132-33
Guidance counselor, 160-61
Guru
    boss/manager, 164
    definition, 147
    friend, 158-59
    parents, 151-55
    siblings, 155-58

teachers, 161-63
you as, 147-51

H
Haste, 186-88
Honesty, 106-12, 237-38

I
Indecision, 180
Initiative, 5
Integrity, 110-12
Intentions, 182-83
Internship, 220-21
Interviews, 167-72
Intuition, 4, 36-41
Inward actions, 243-47

J-L
Journal, 131-34
Karma, 197-98
Lessons, 133
Lethargy, 181
Living options, 20-22

M
Meal plans, 21
Meditation, 206-7, 209
Mentors
    finding, 159-64
    guidance counselor, 160-61
    professional organizations, 163
    teachers, 161-63

N
Nonclinging approach, 241-43
Nonharming approach, 235-36
Nonstealing approach, 238-40
Nutrition, 177-80

O
Obstacles
    bigger picture, 194-202
    exhaustion, 176-80
    fear, 195-202
    getting stuck, 188-90
    haste, 186-88

overconfidence, 191-94
resistance, 180-83
stress, 176-80
Orientation outings, 249-55
Outward actions, 235-43

P-Q

Parents, 26-27, 151-55
Procrastination, 180
Quality of life, 20-23
Quiet time, 179-80
Quotes, 134

R

Reading, 134
Recommendations, 164-67
Recruitment events, 15
Reflection, 246-47
Rejection, 204-5, 212-16, 221-22
Resistance, 180-86
Roommate, 20-21

S

School choice
academic life, 30-33
competition, 48-52
culture, 16-19
diversity factors, 13-16
extracurriculars, 23-26
financial aid, 26-30
geography, 8-13
intuition, 36-41
living options, 20-22
personal goals, 47-48
process, 1-4
quality of life, 20-23
research, 33-36
size considerations, 4-8
tuition costs and, 27
weather, 11-13
School visit, 34-35
Self awareness, 55-57
Self-care, 150-51
Self-discovery, 125-29
Self-protection, 119-20

Self-study, 101-3
Service, 89-97
Siblings, 155-58
Size
extracurricular
considerations, 5-6
pros/cons, 4-5
questions to consider, 7-8
social issues, 6
Sleep, 178
Social life, 6
Social scene, 17-18
Sororities, 17
Stress, 176-80
Student representatives, 34

T

Talents. *See* Gifts
Teachers, 161-63
Time off, 216-19, 222-25
To-do-list
inward actions, 243-47
outward actions, 235-43
Topography, 11-12
Transfers, 225-28
Trustworthiness, 237-38

V

Values
in action, 87-88
application, 89
awareness exercise, 80-89
definition, 78
identification, 82-83
importance of, 78-79
sample, 85
View books, 34

W

Waiting period, 203-8
Weather, 11-13
Websites, 34
Wheel of life, 148-49
Work-study programs, 27-28
Writer, 136-37